AF323671

JEFF BURTON

The Other Place

TWIN PALMS PUBLISHERS 2005

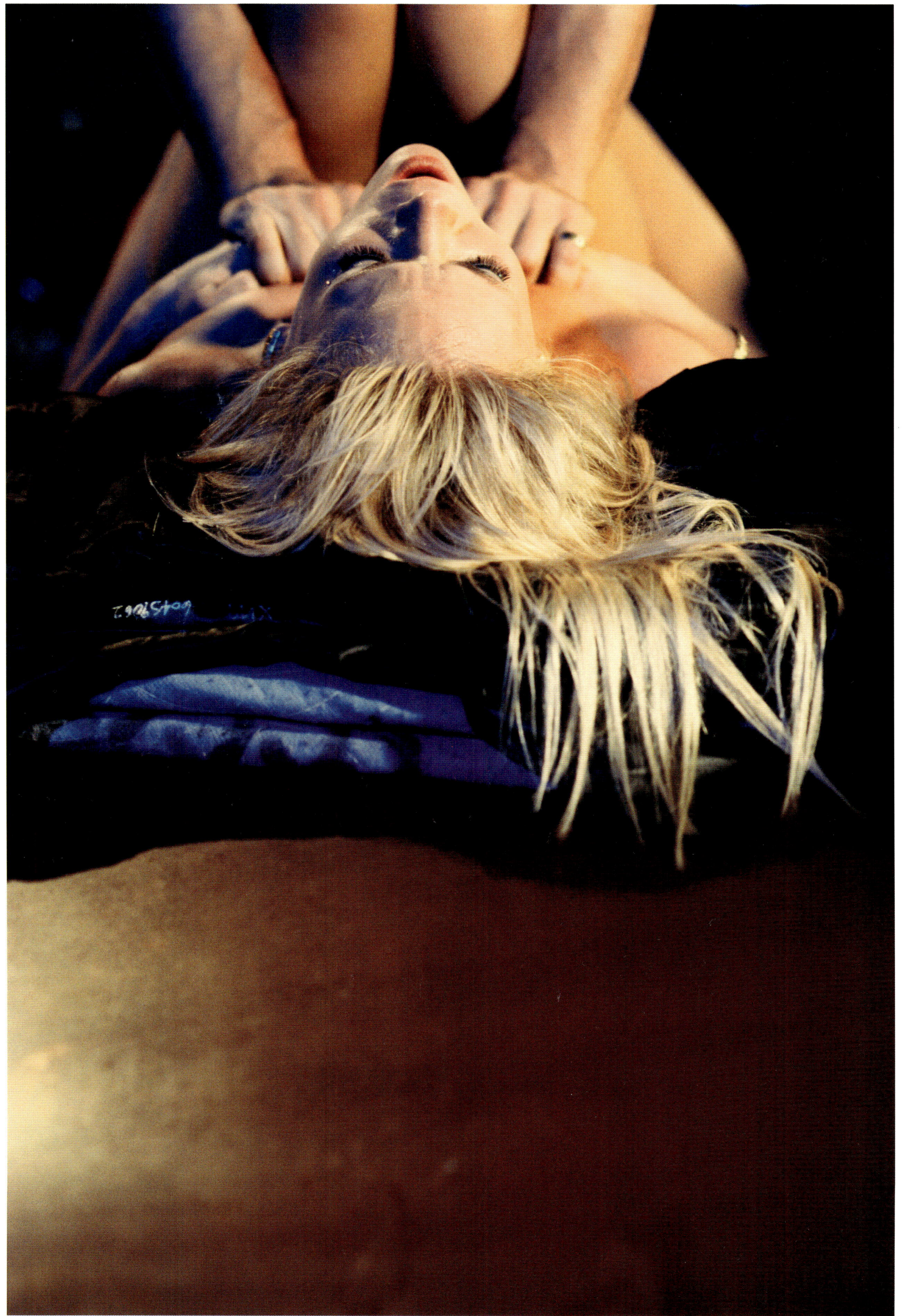

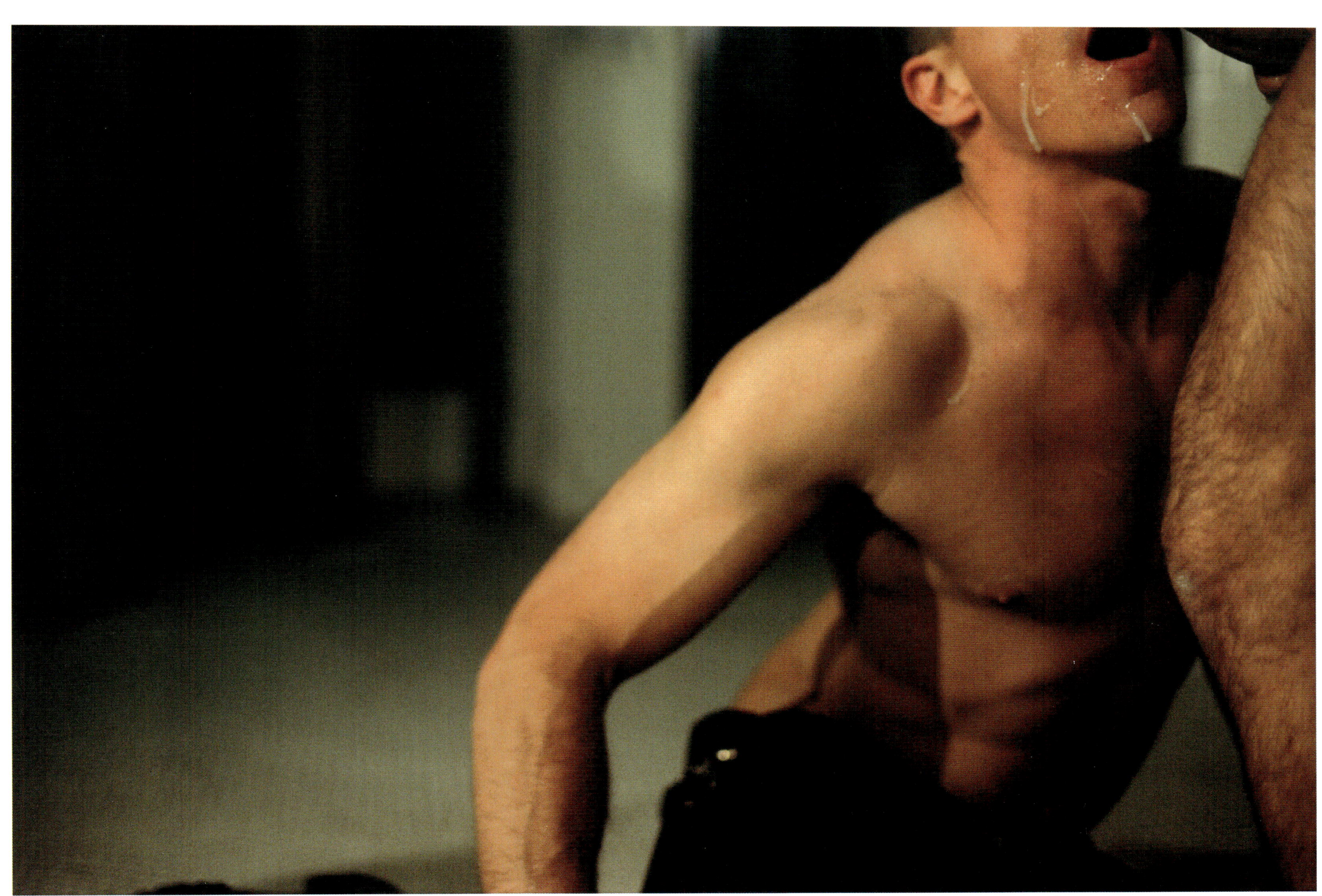

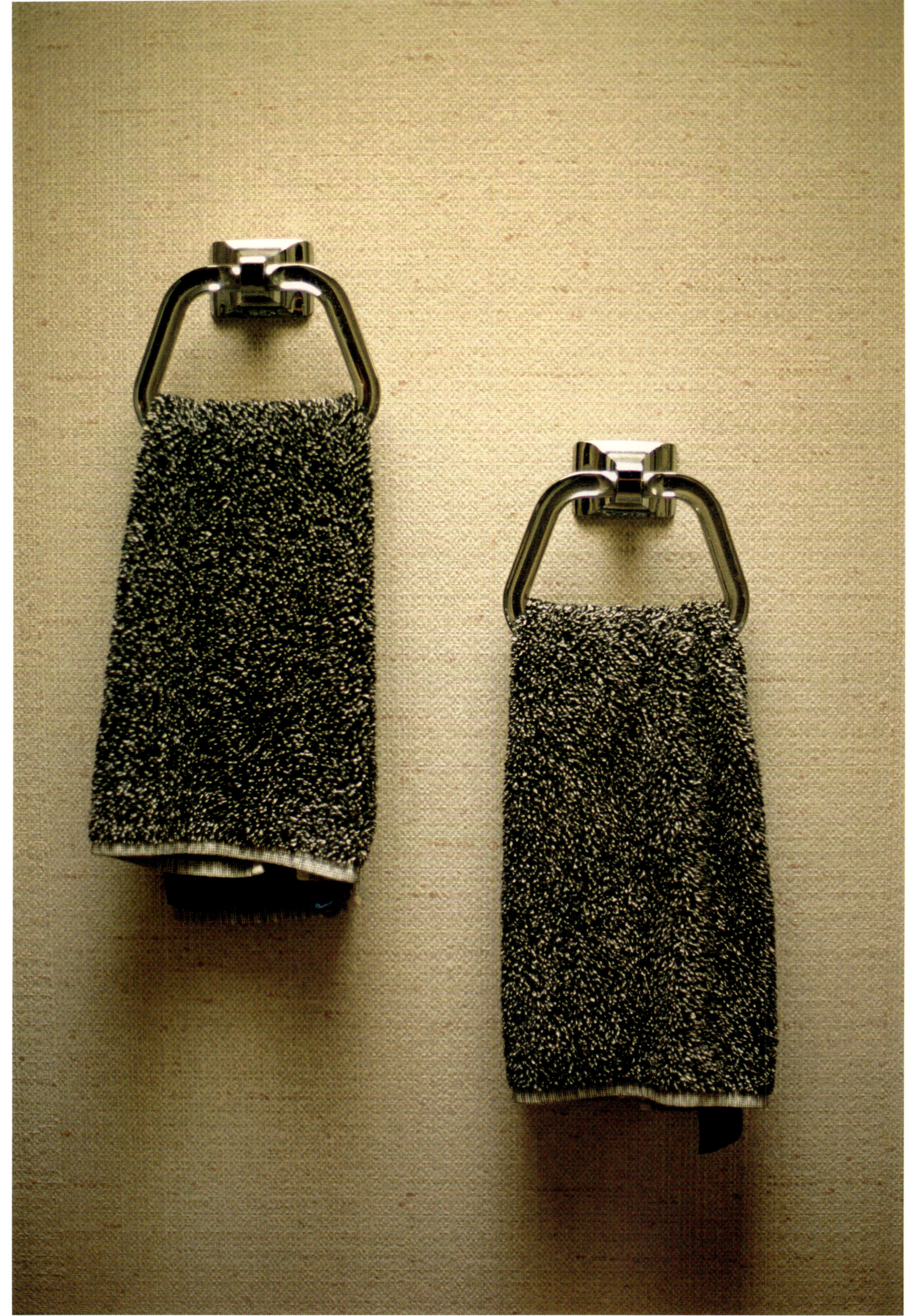

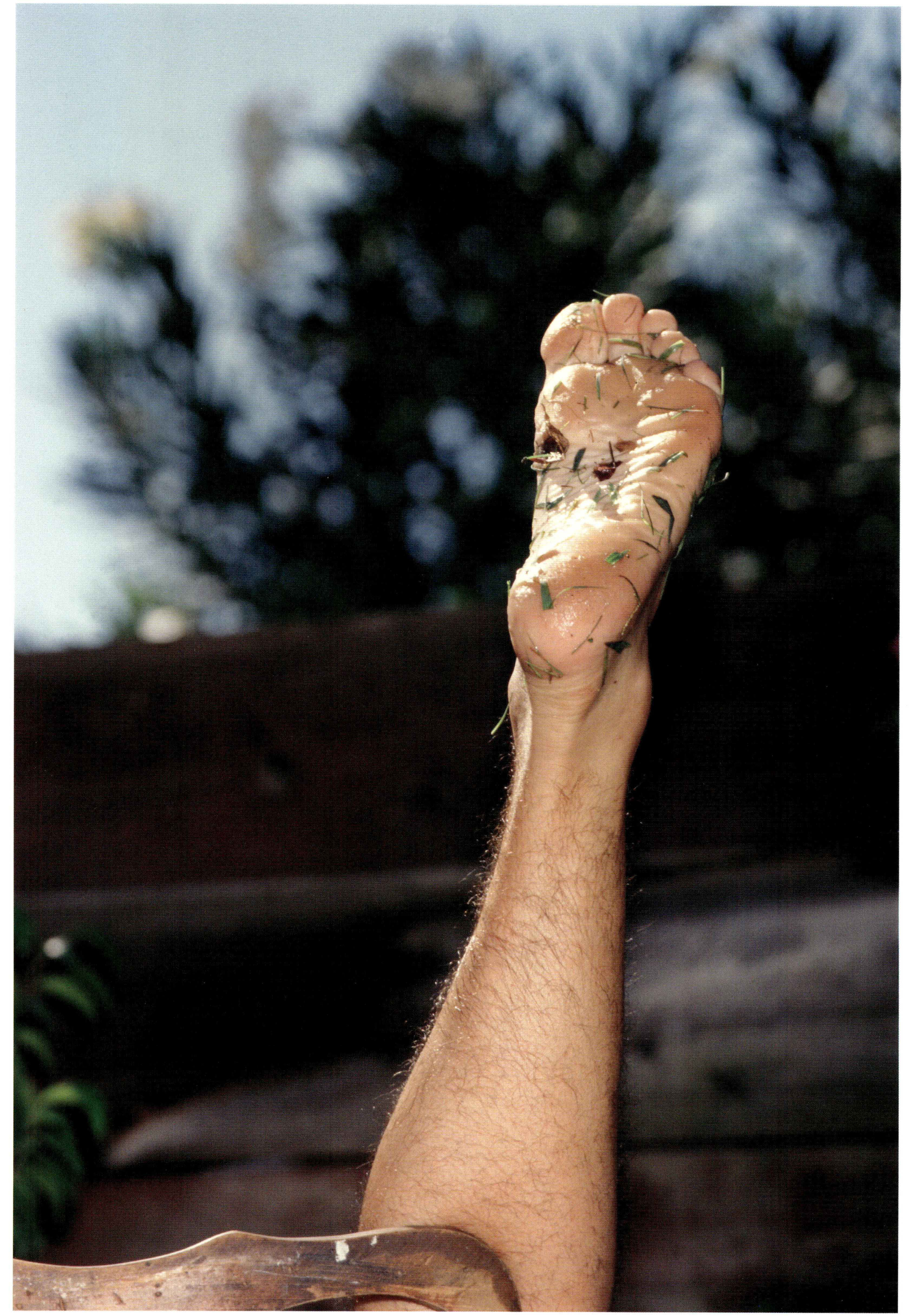

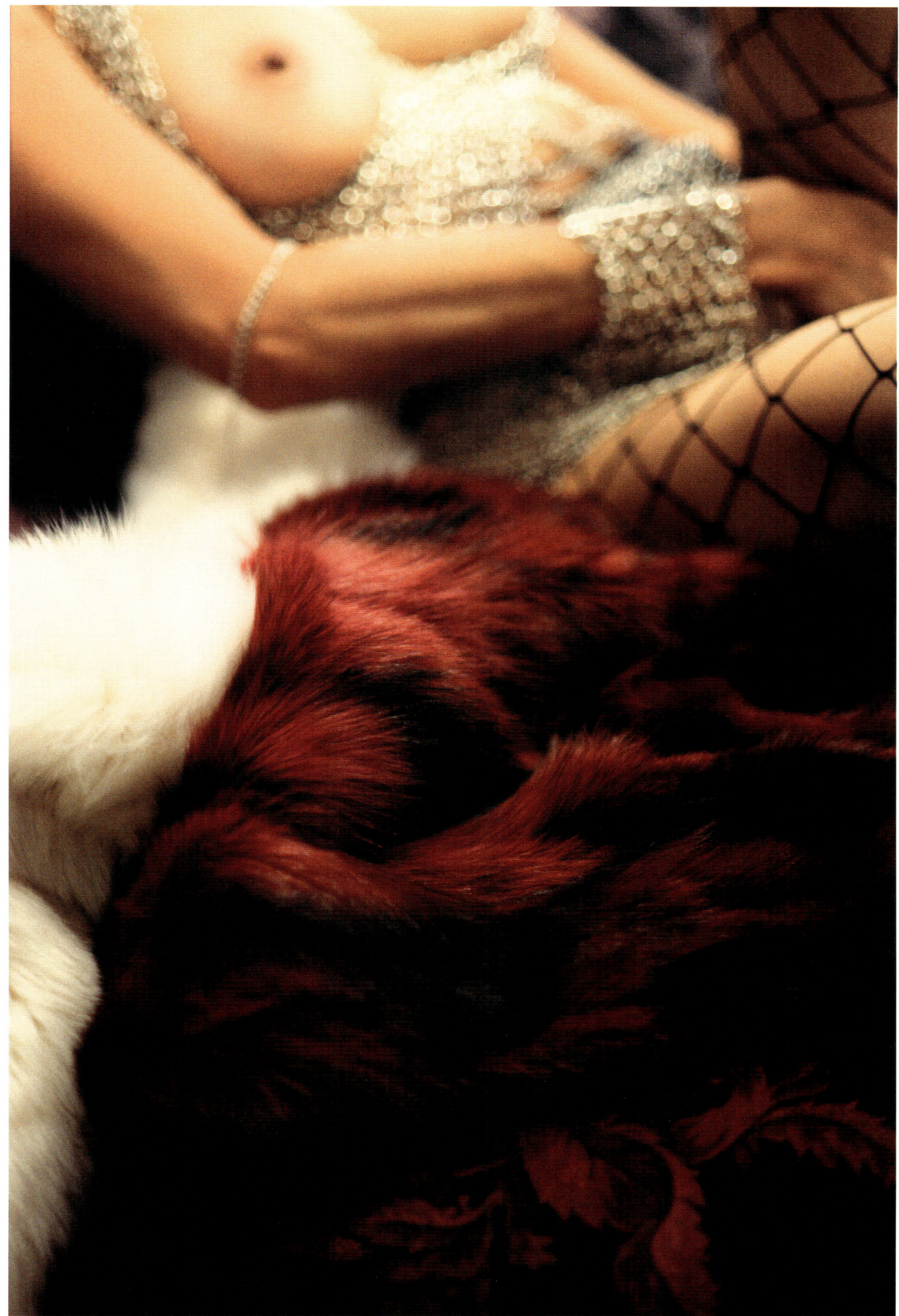

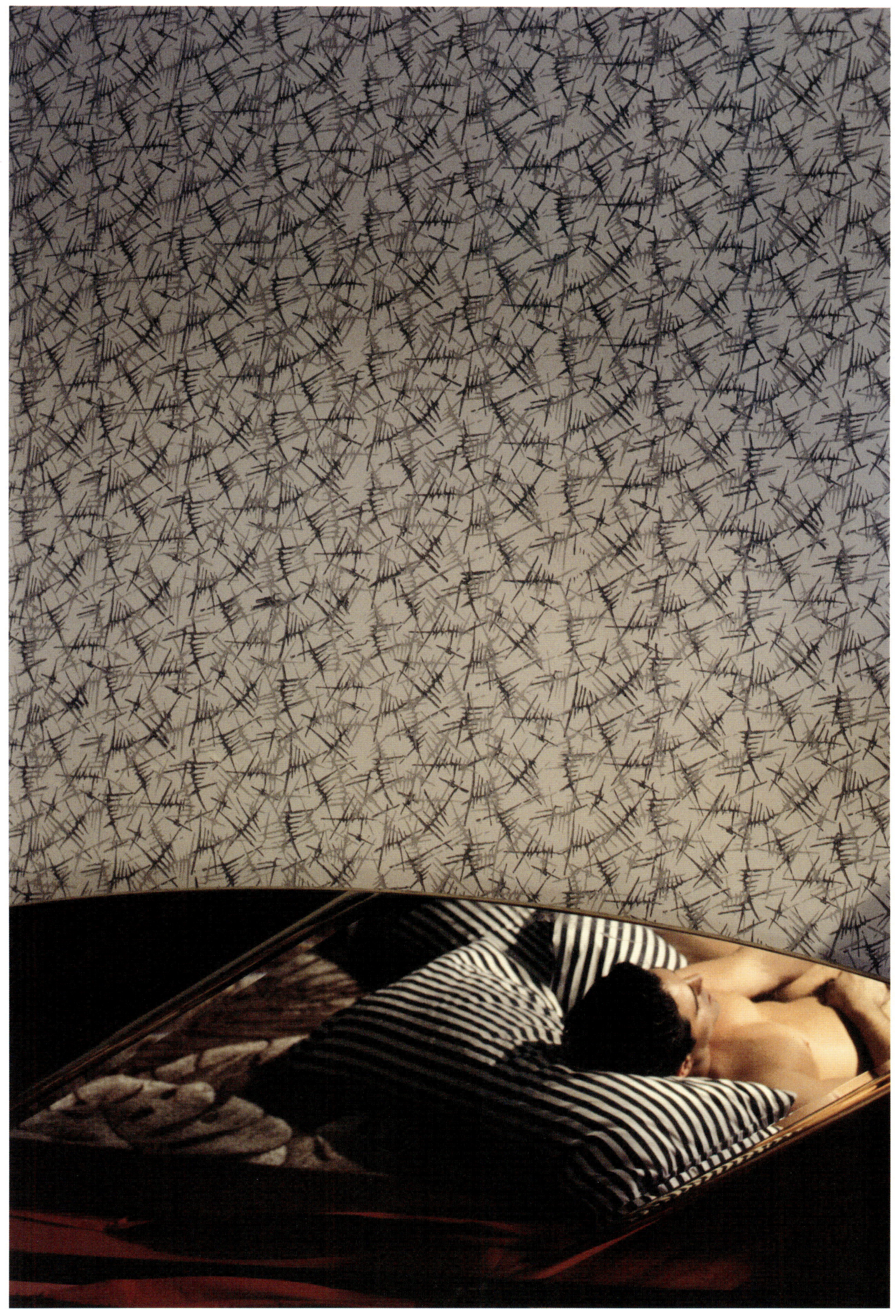

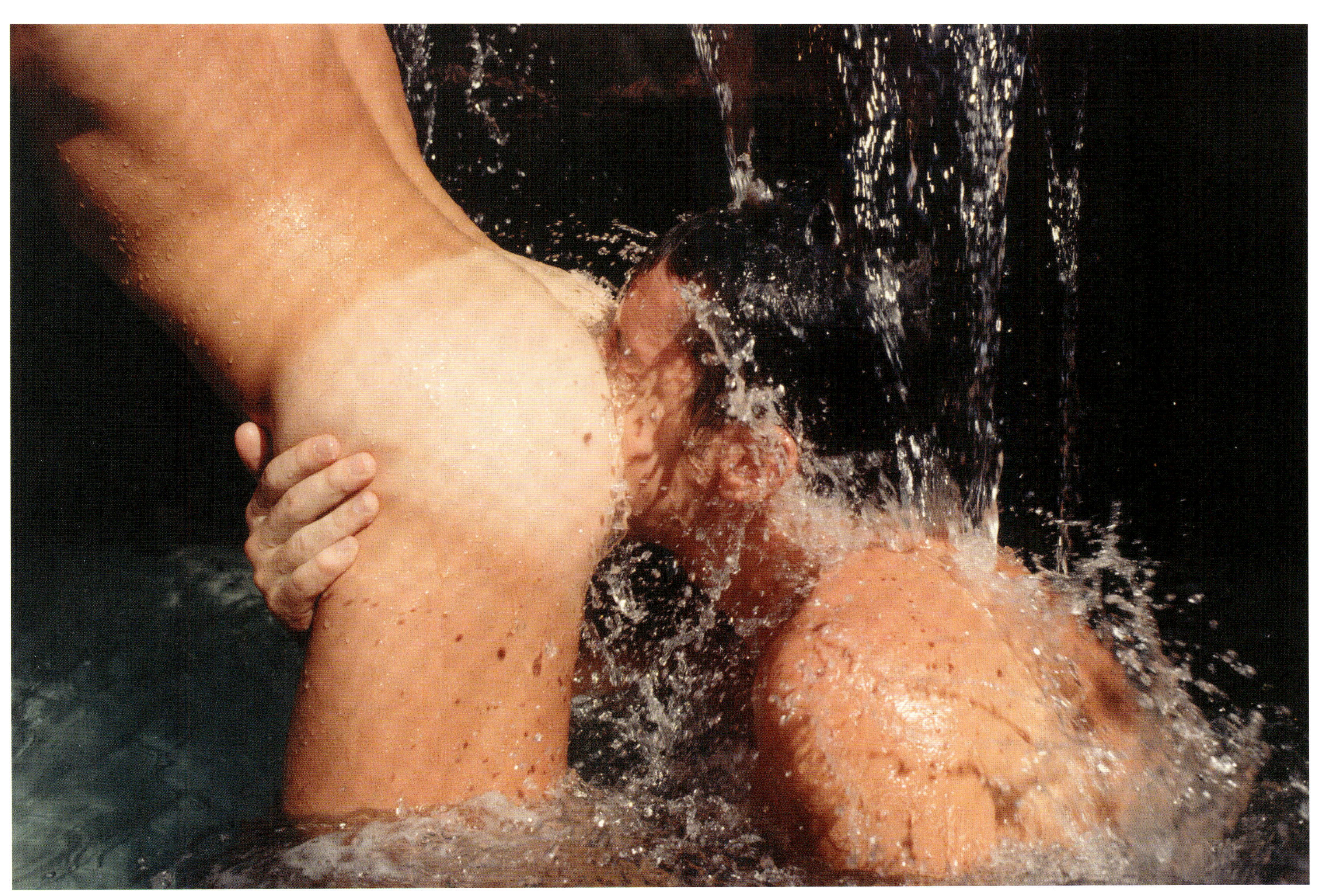

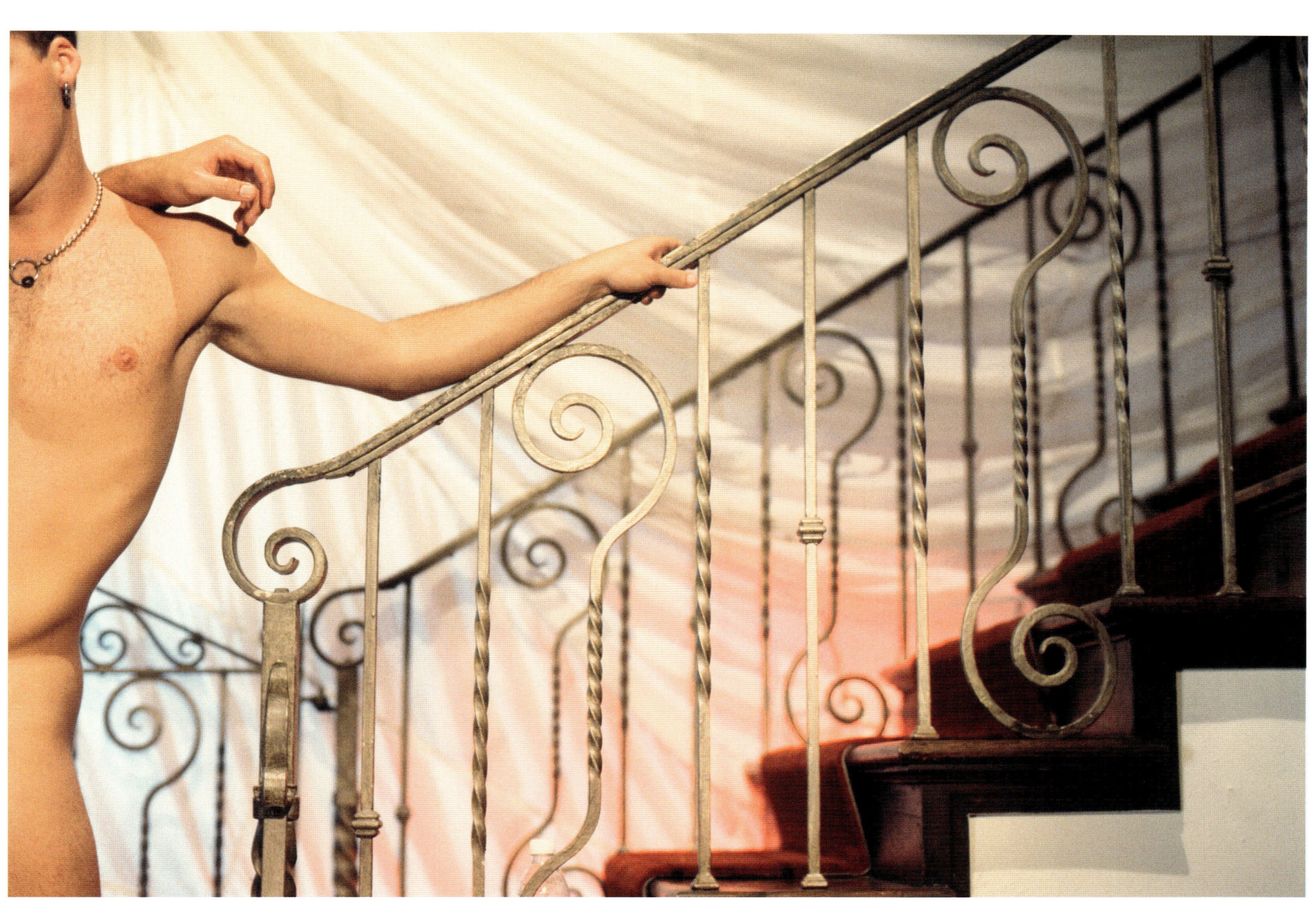

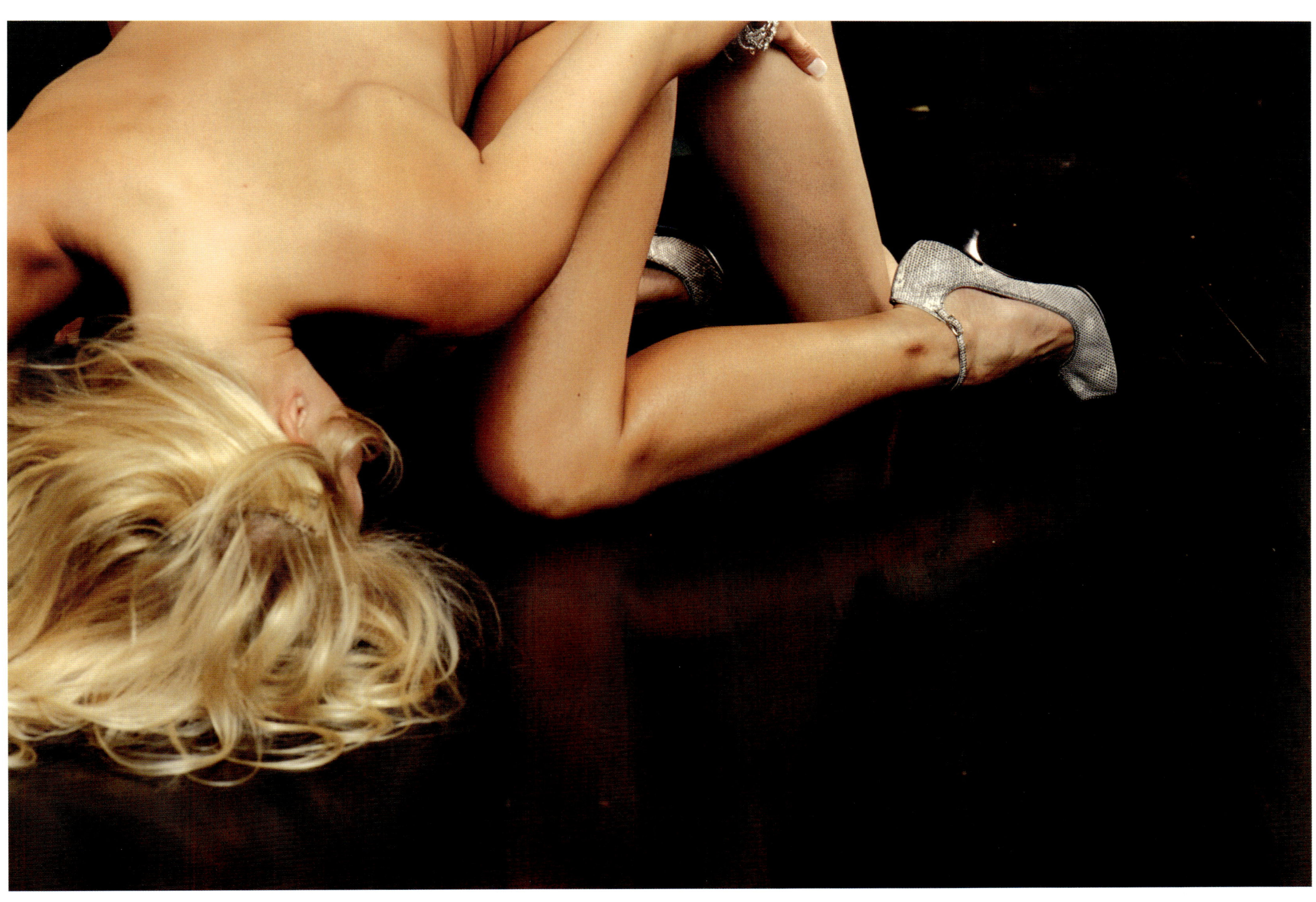

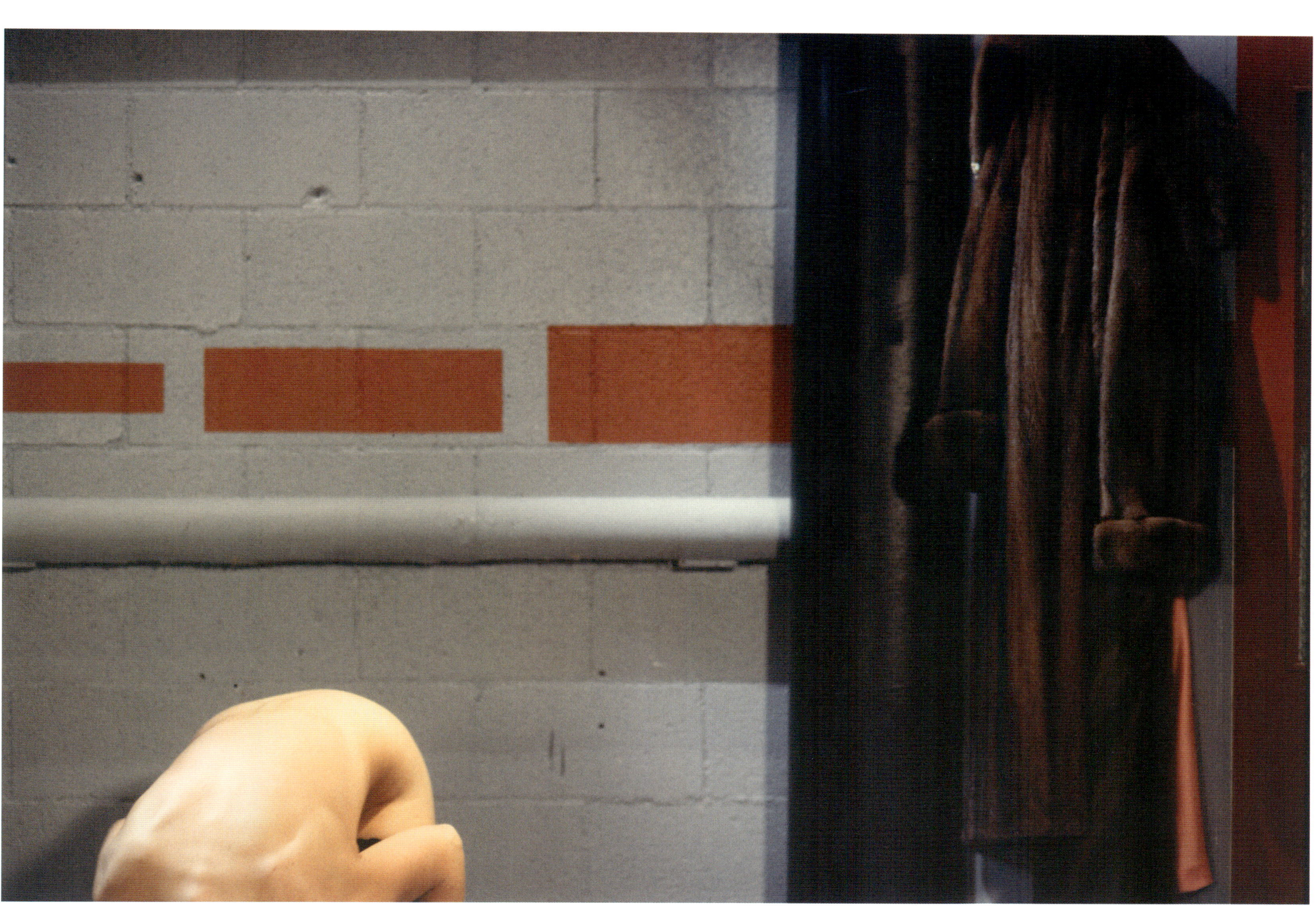

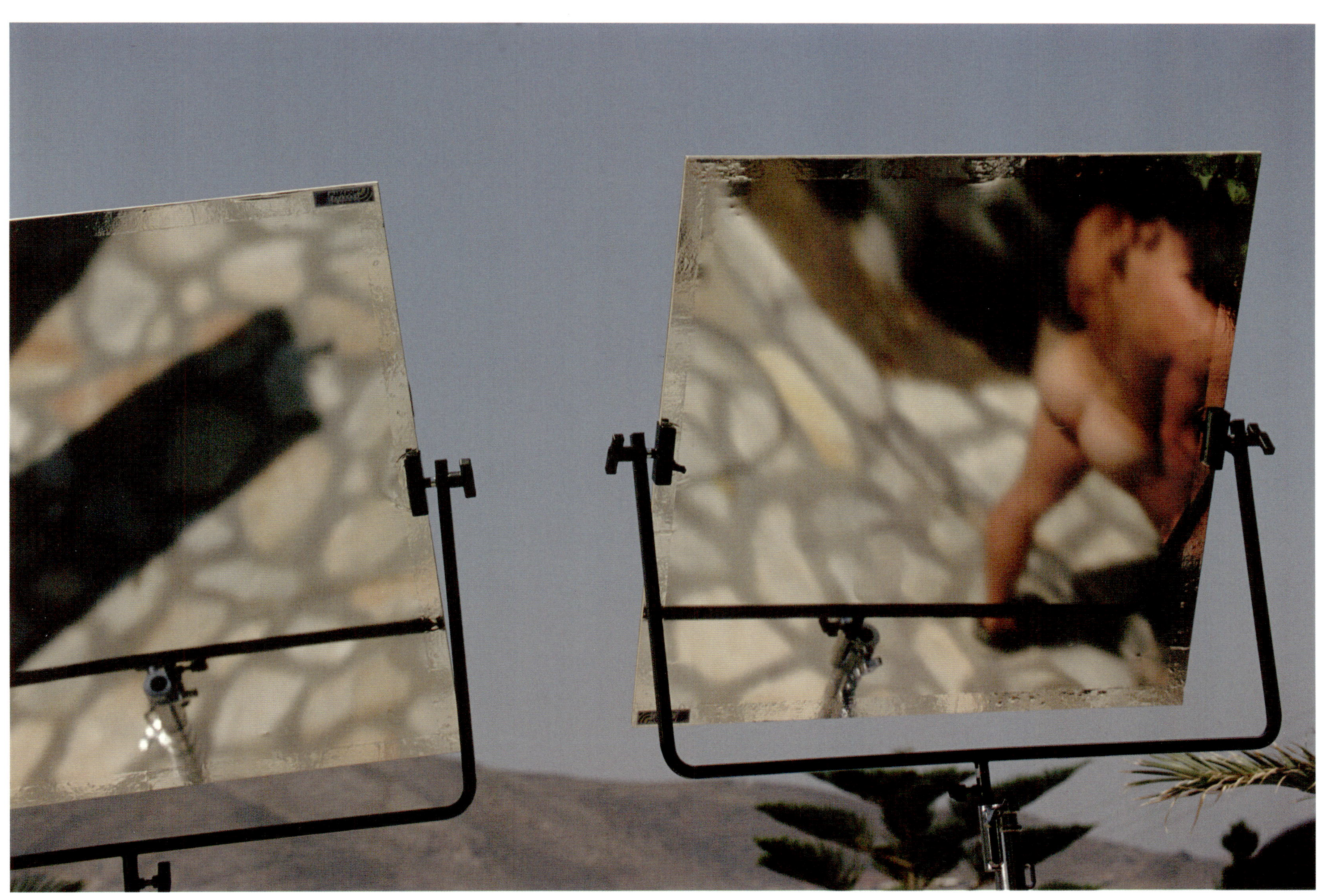

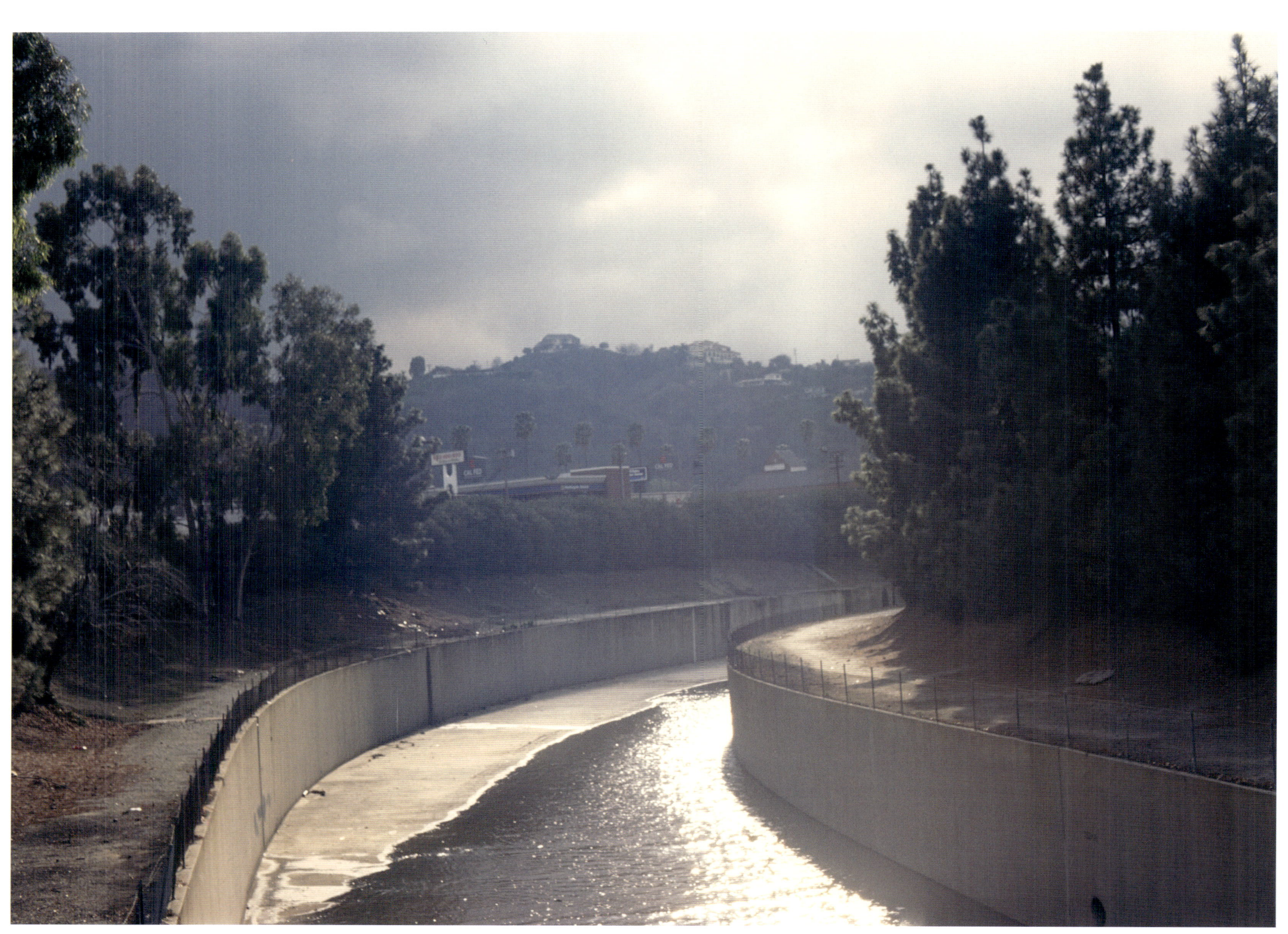

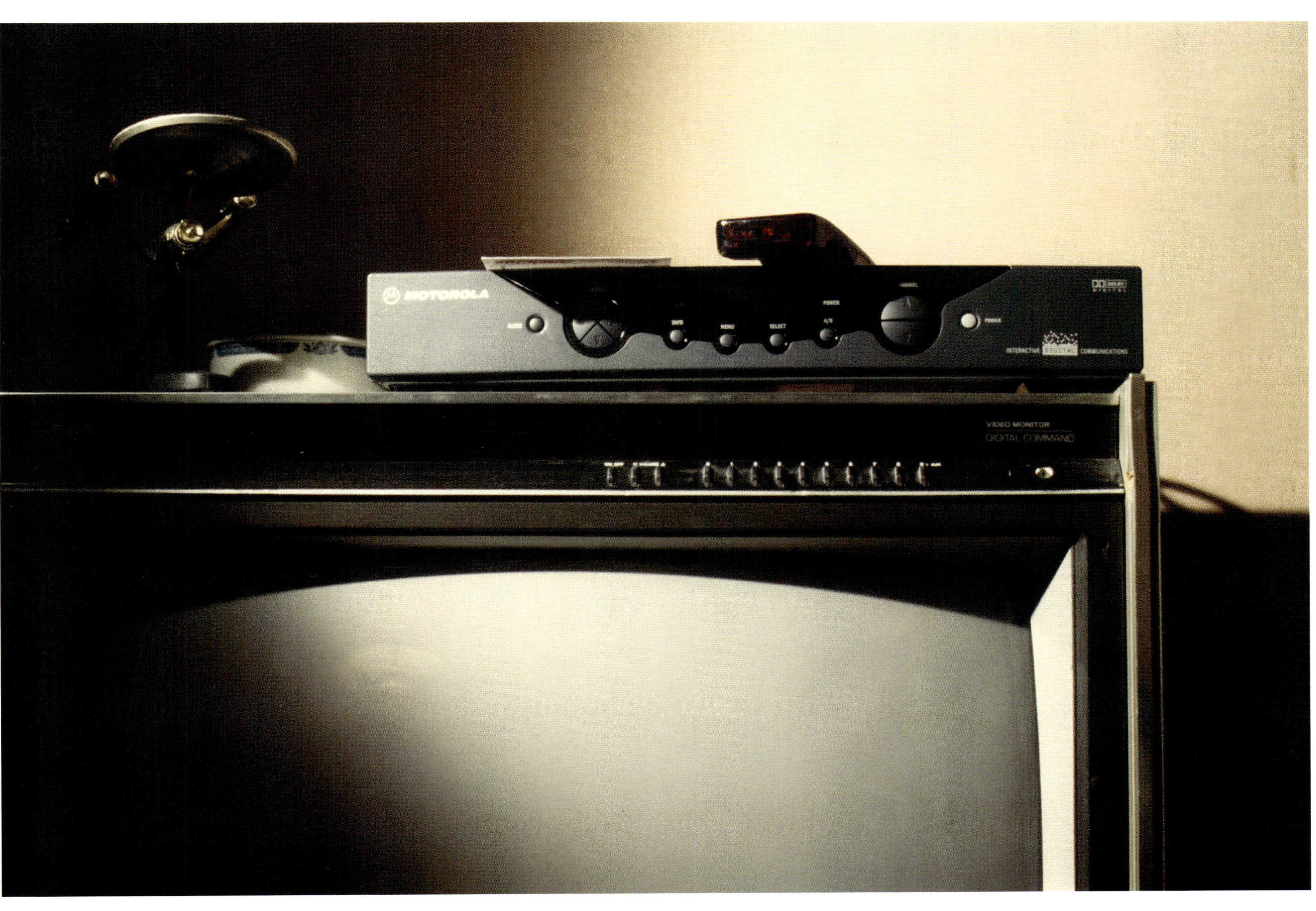

MOTOROLA
DOLBY DIGITAL
INFO   MENU   SELECT   POWER A/B   CHANNEL   POWER
INTERACTIVE DIGITAL COMMUNICATIONS
VIDEO MONITOR
DIGITAL COMMAND

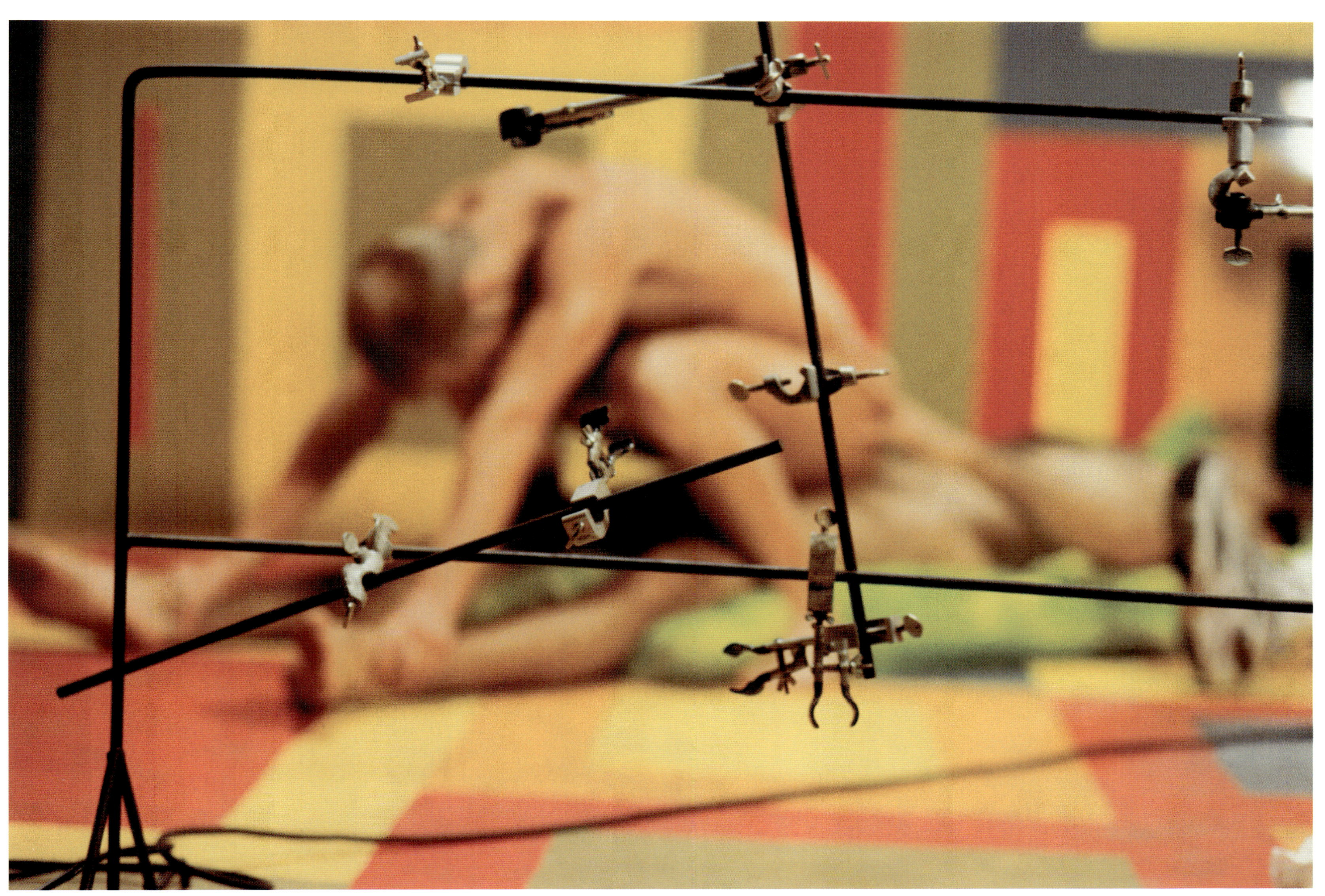

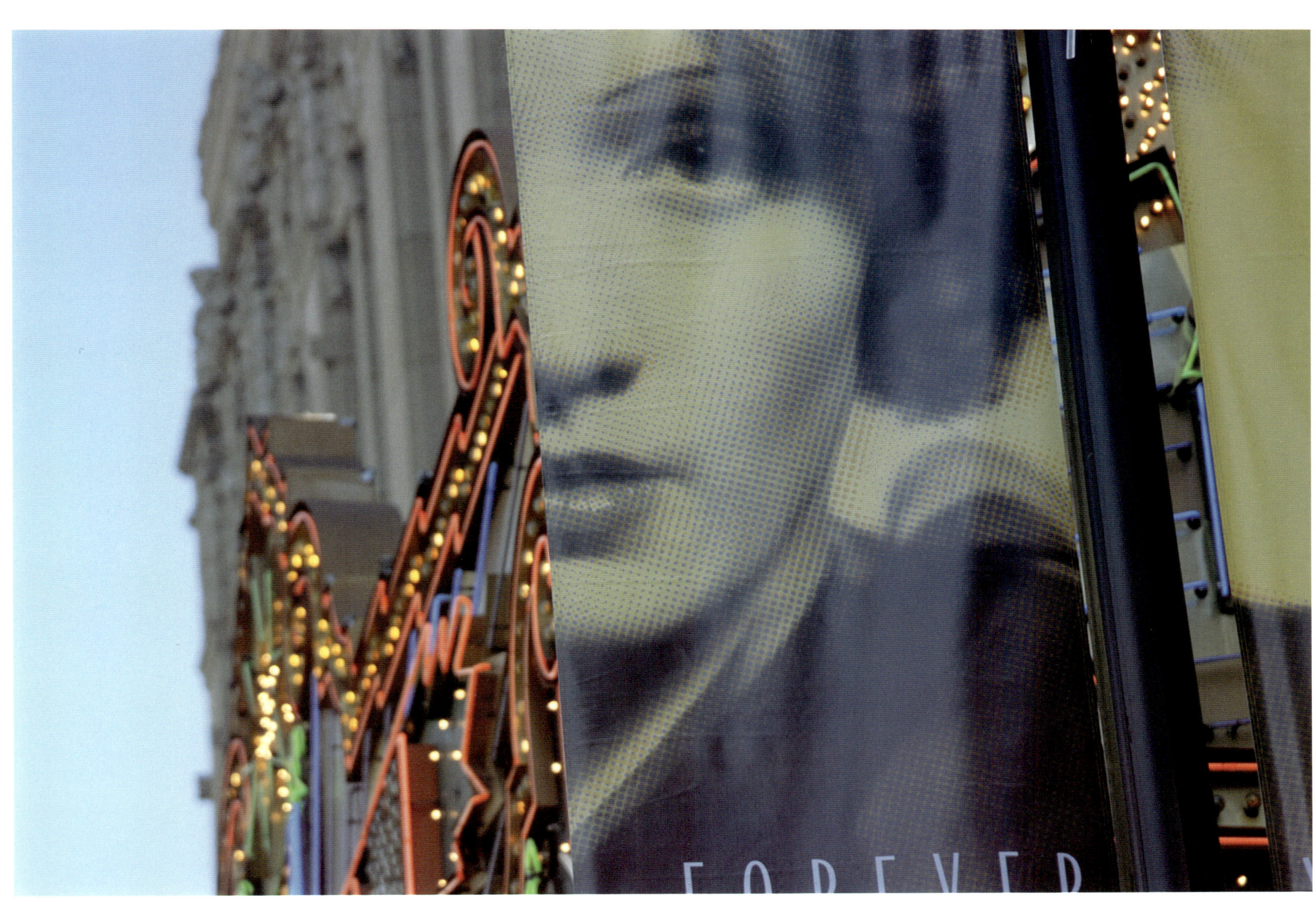

FOREVER

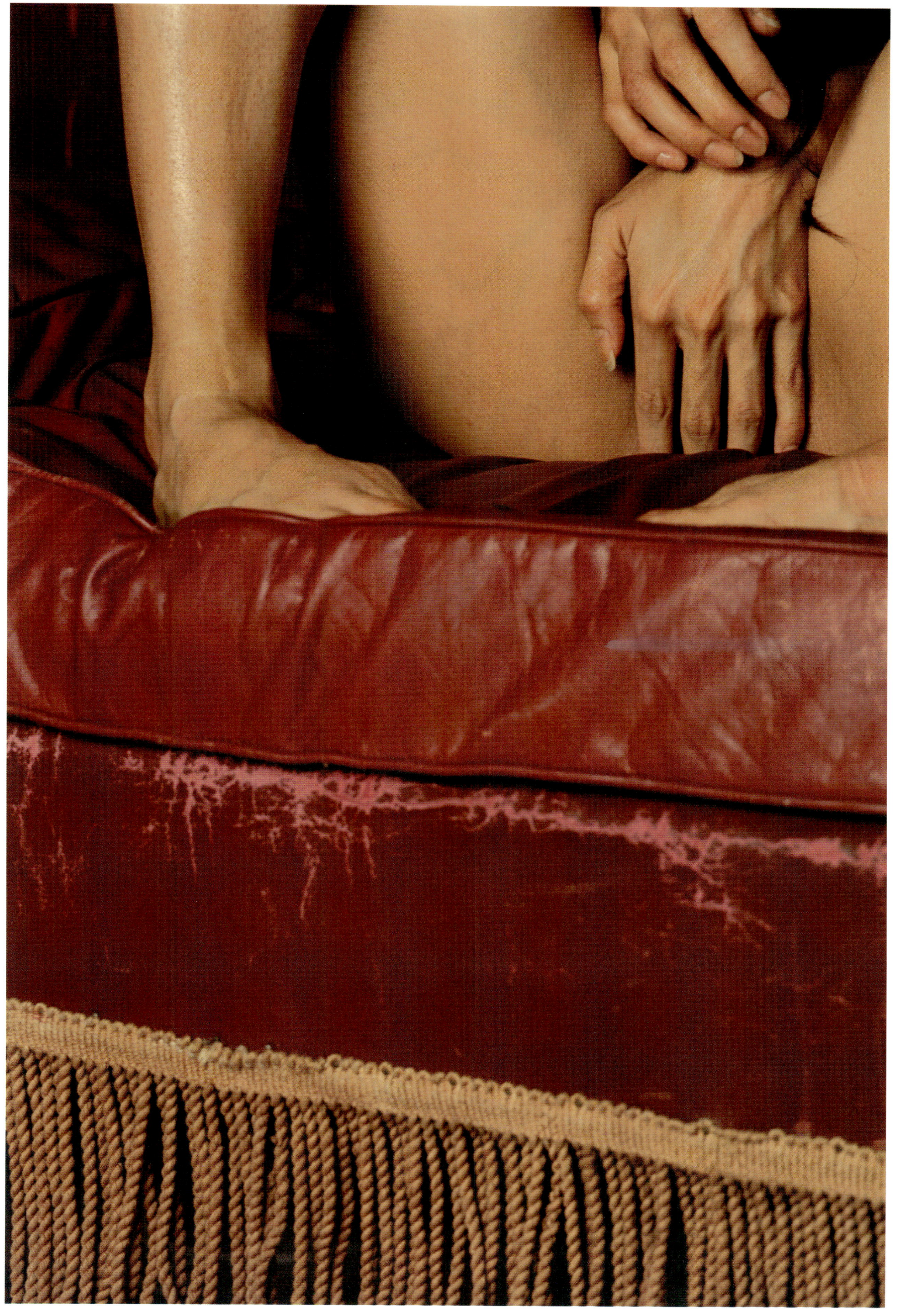

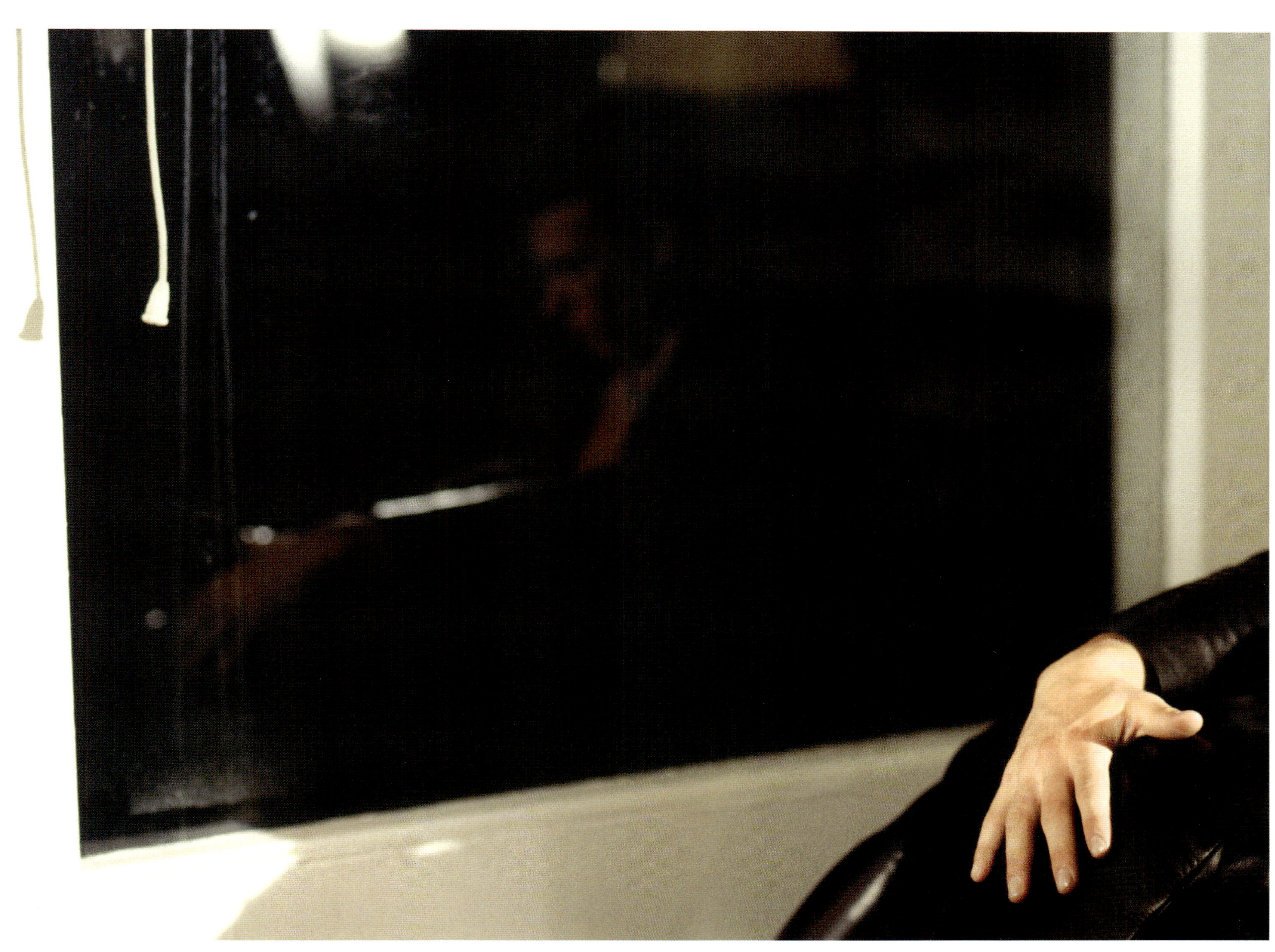

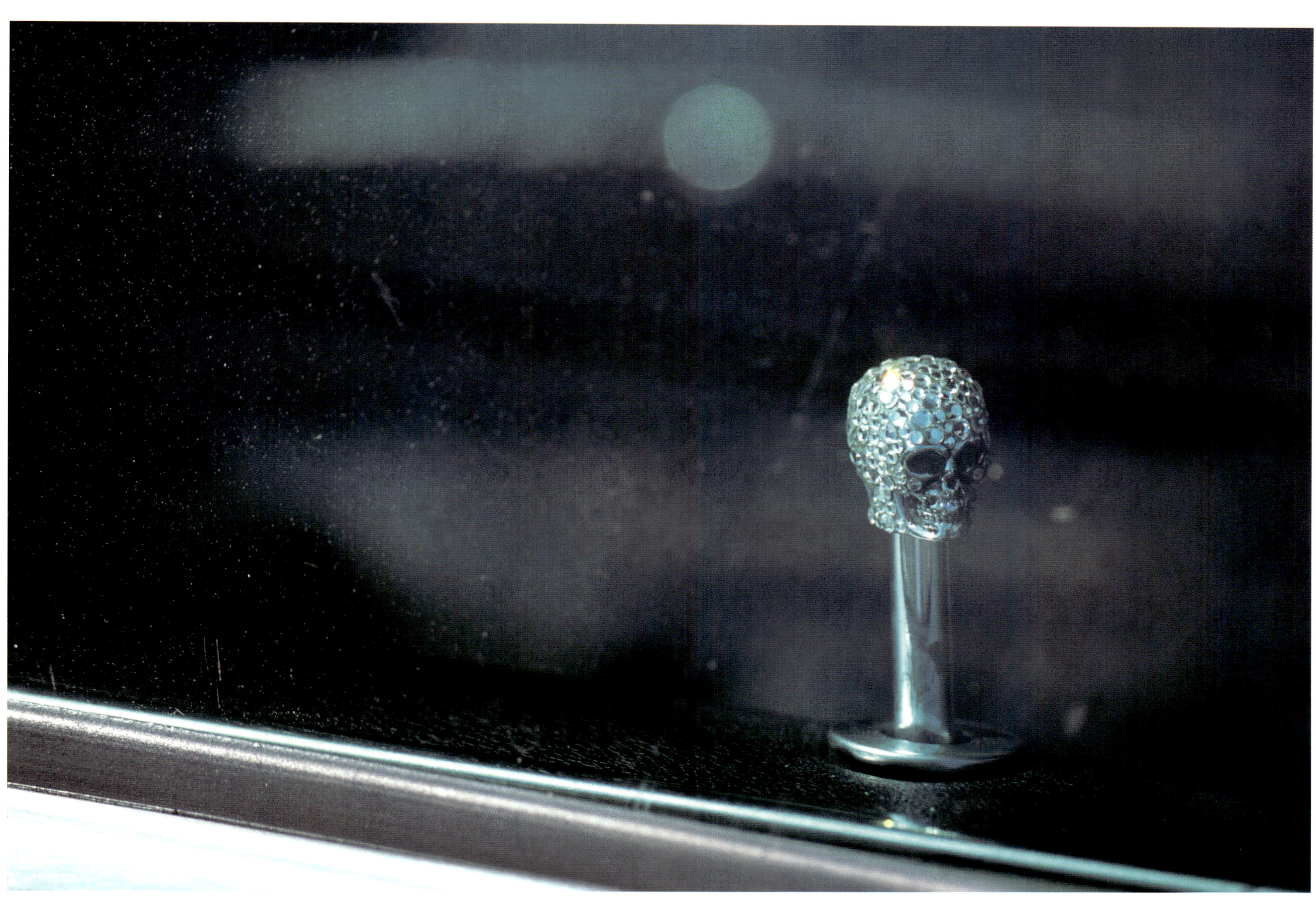

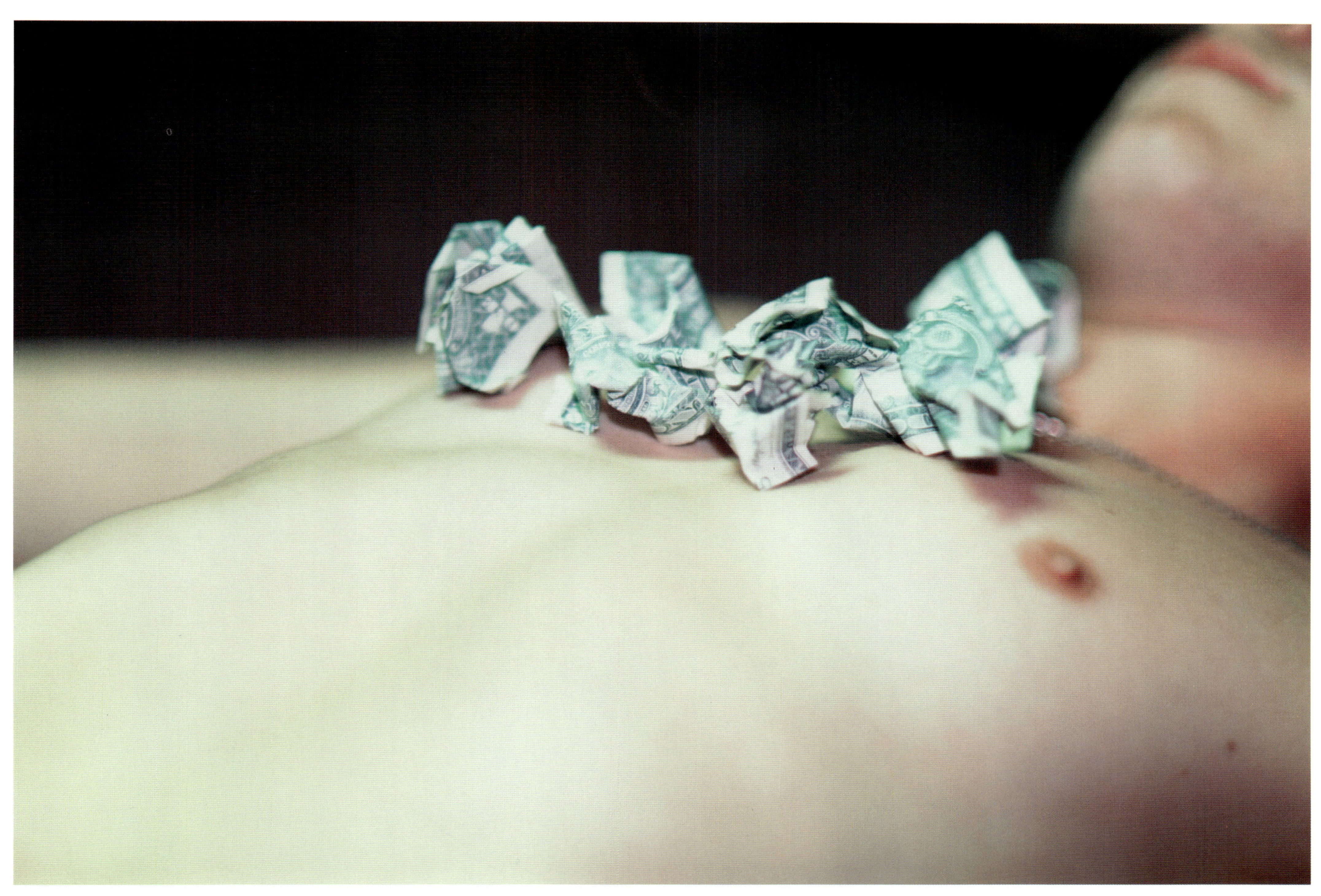

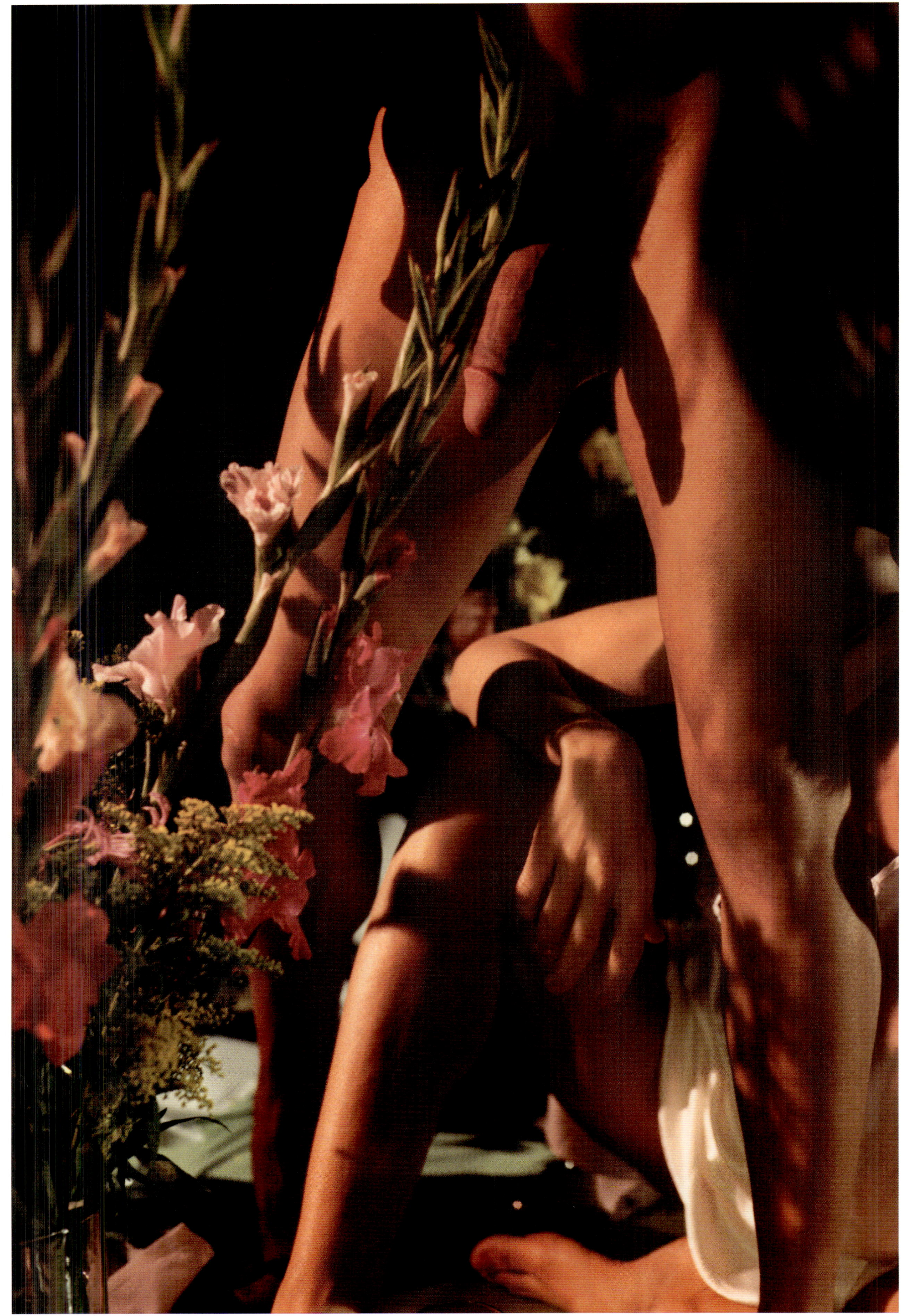

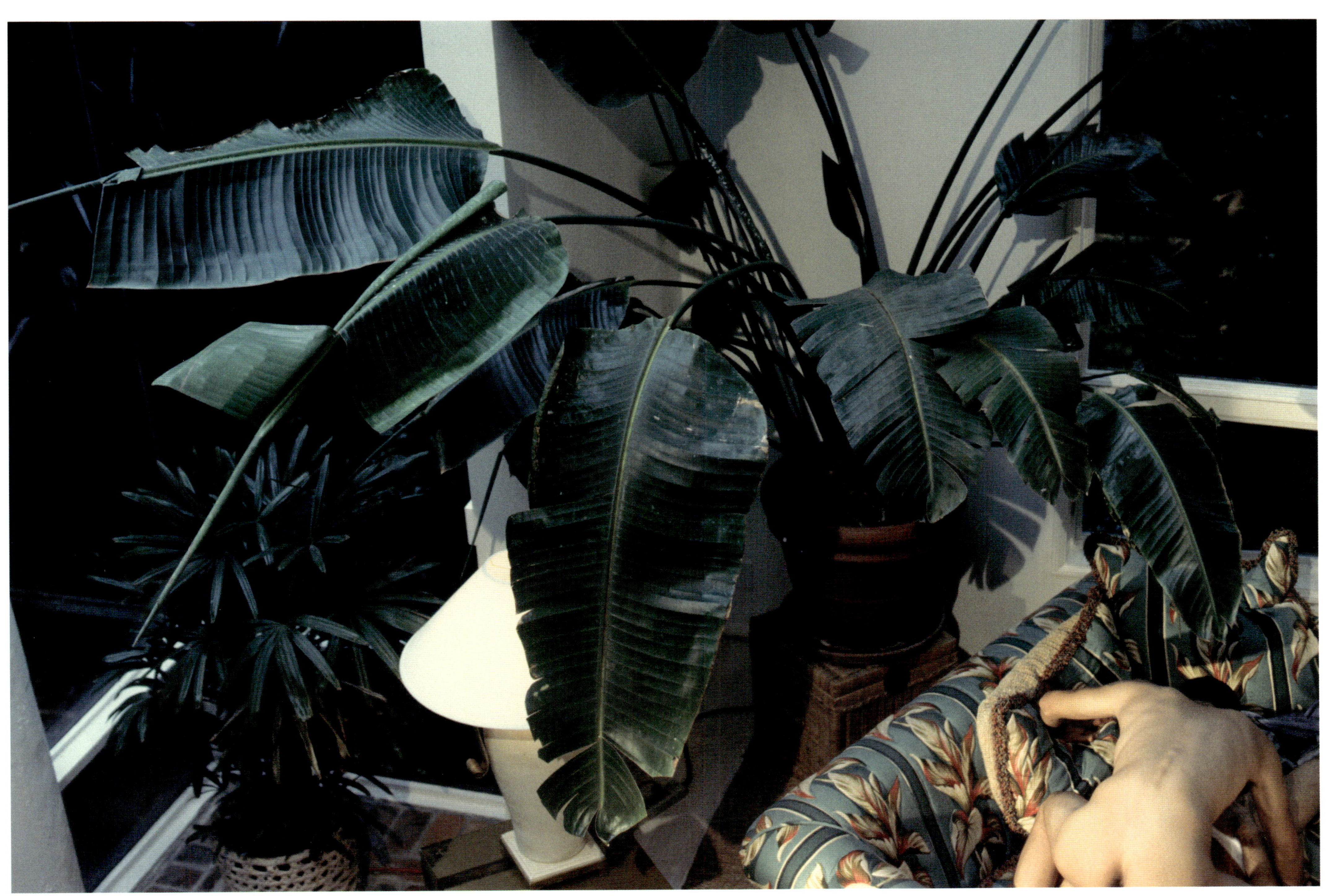

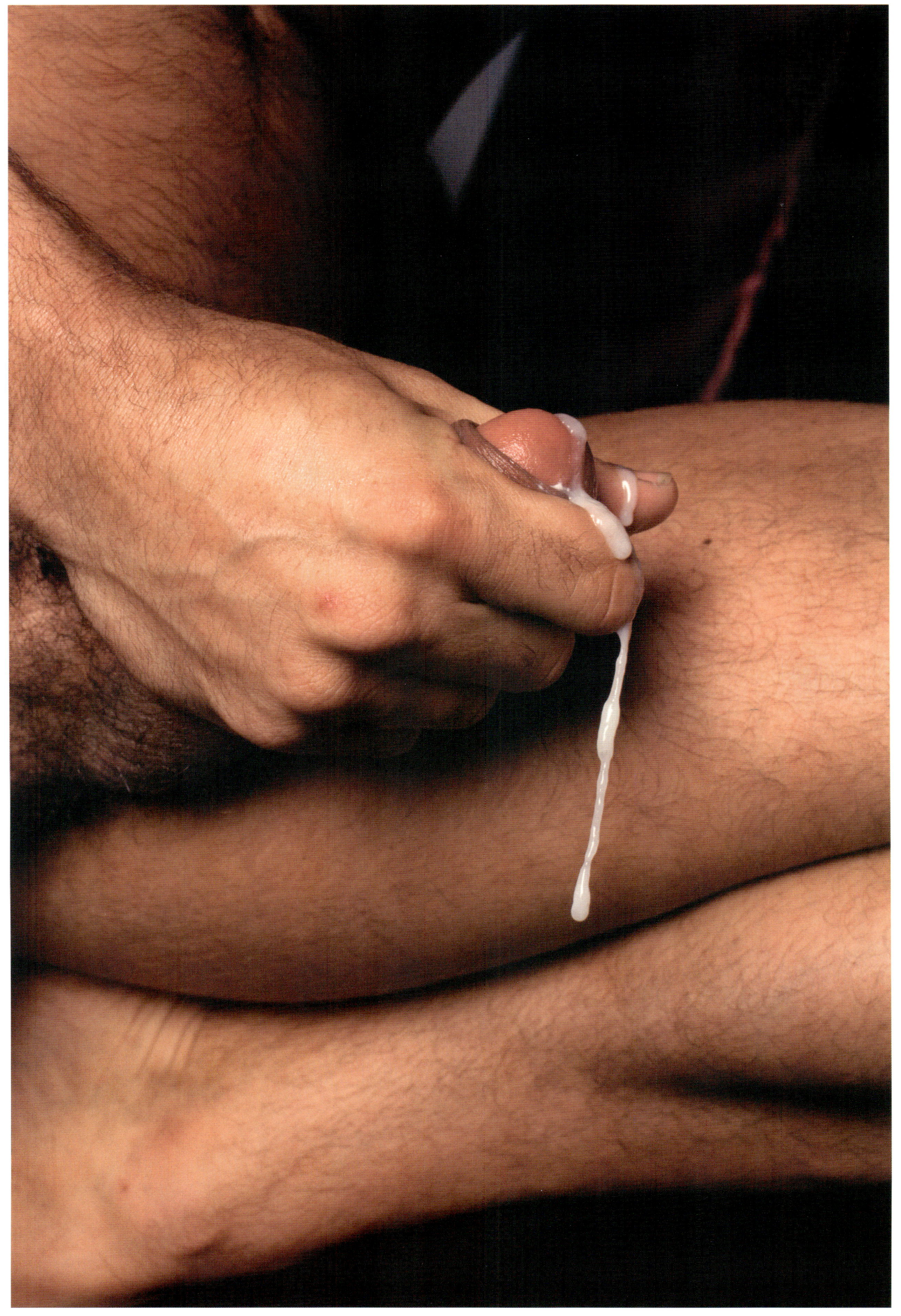

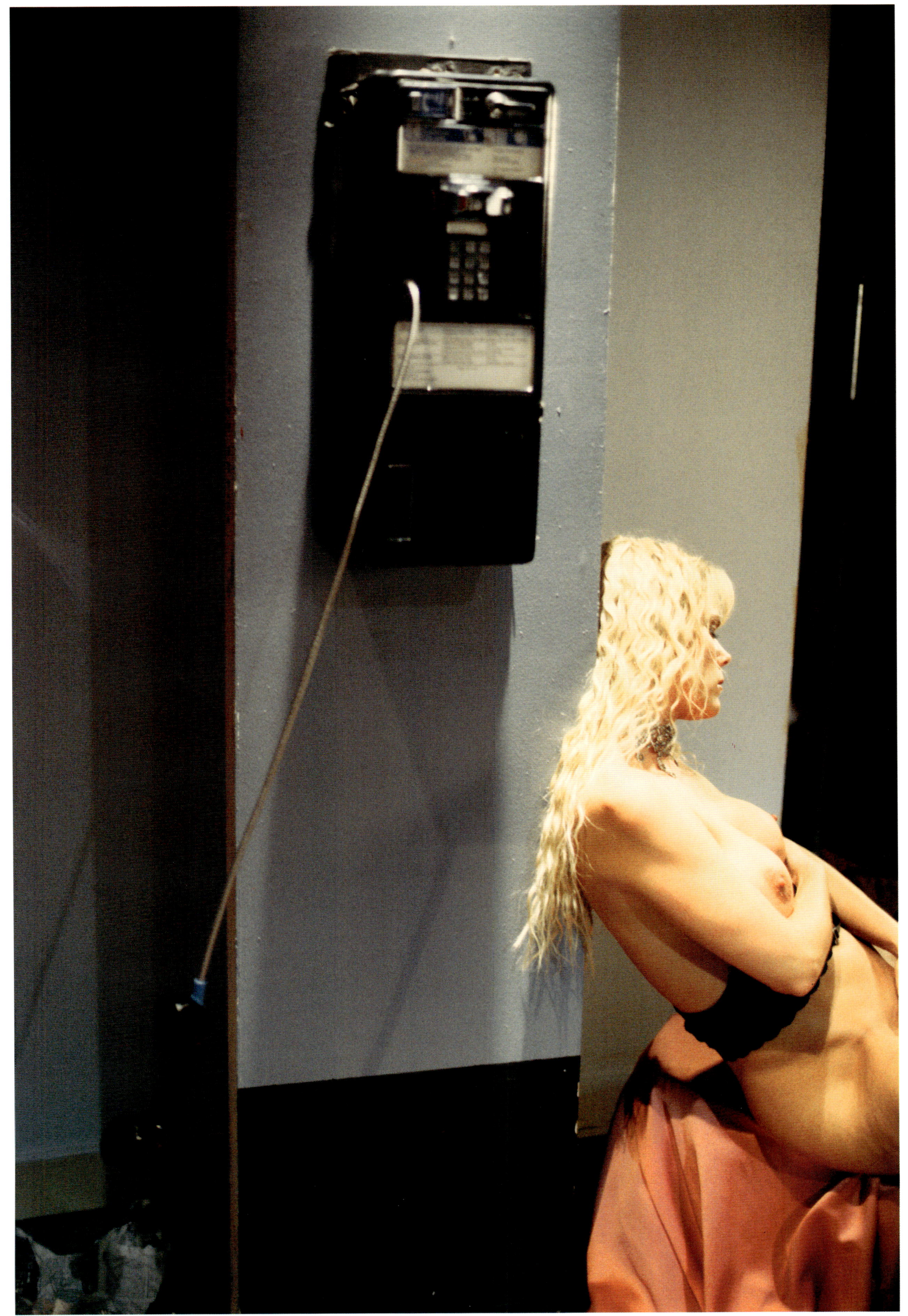

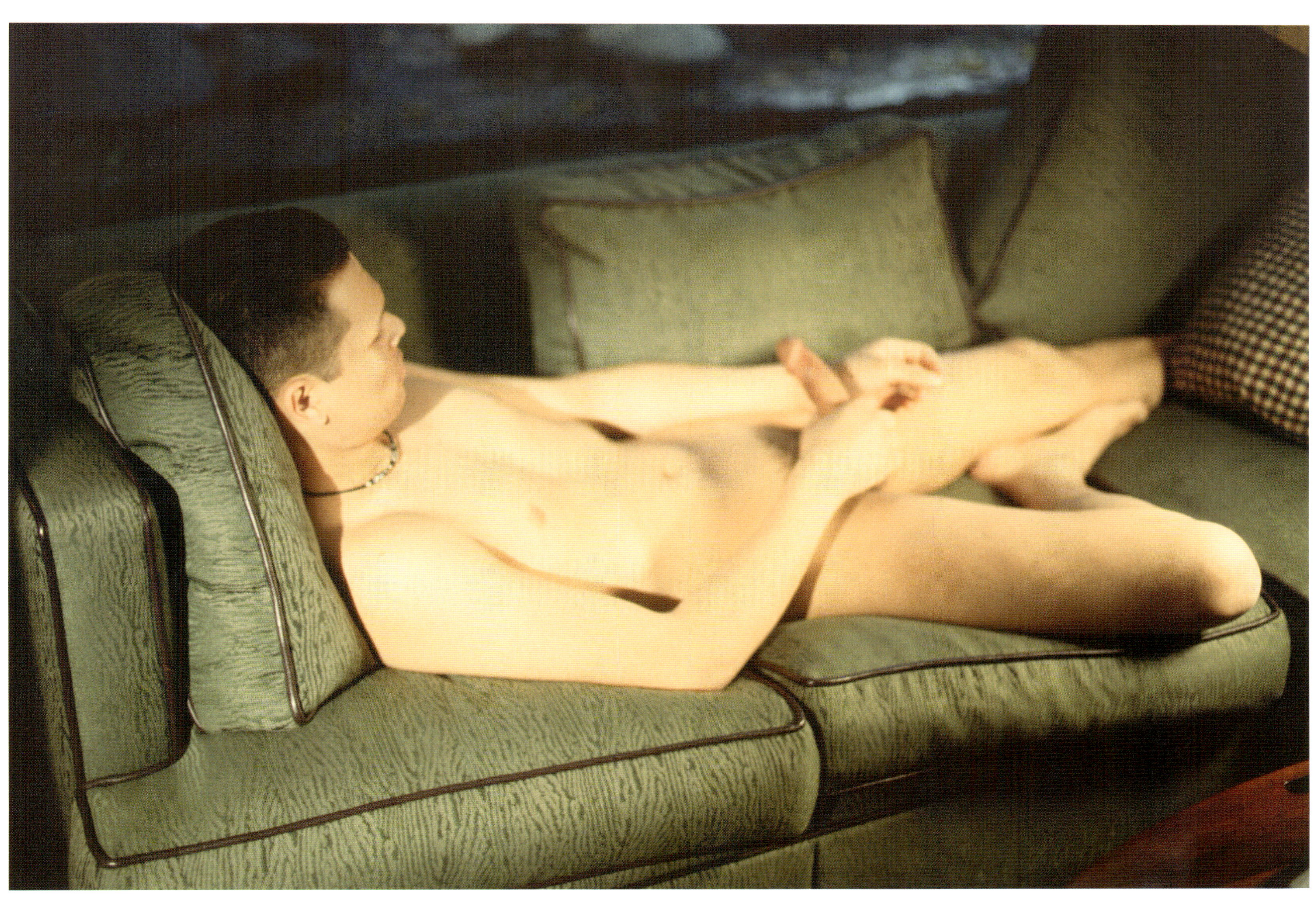

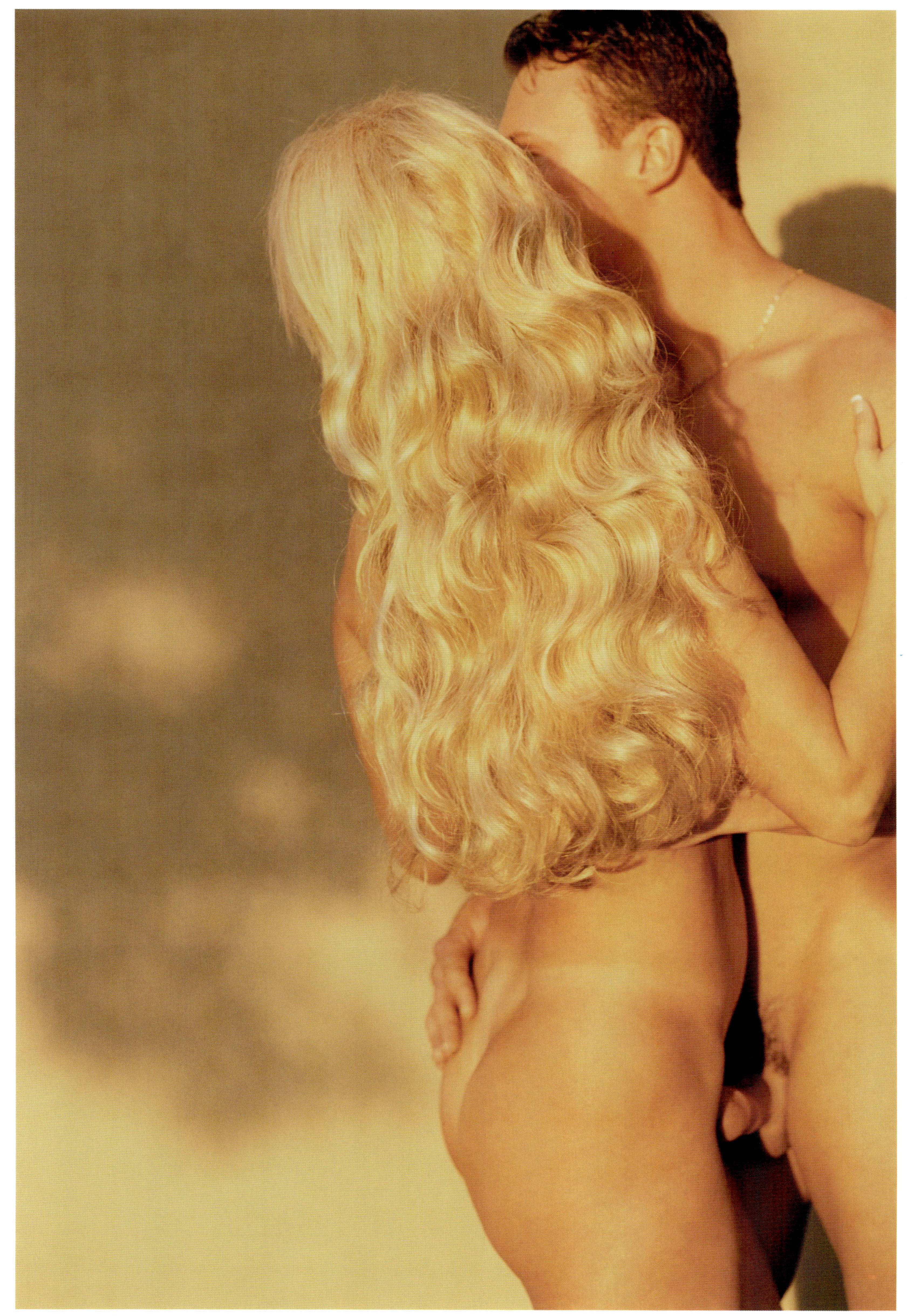

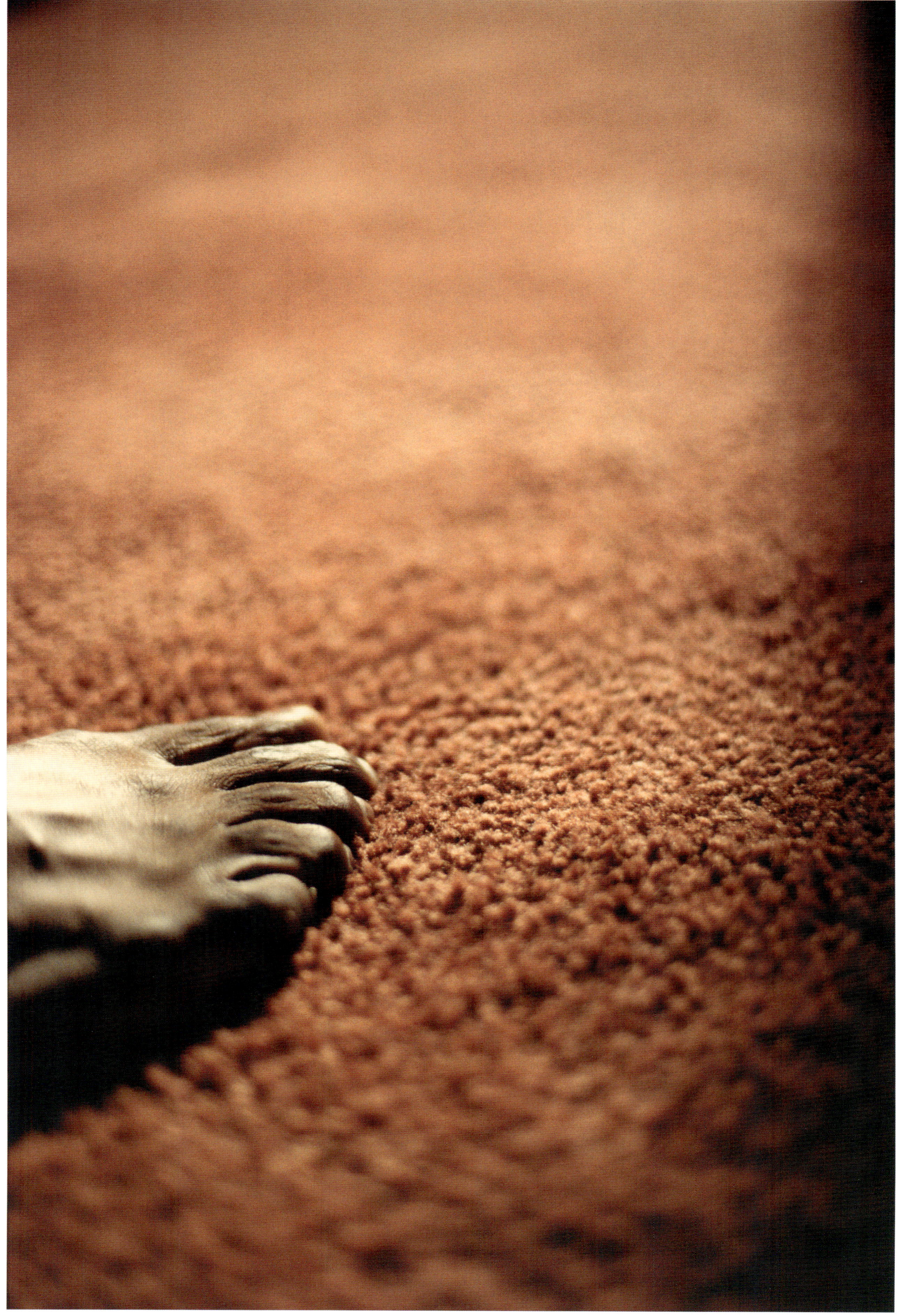

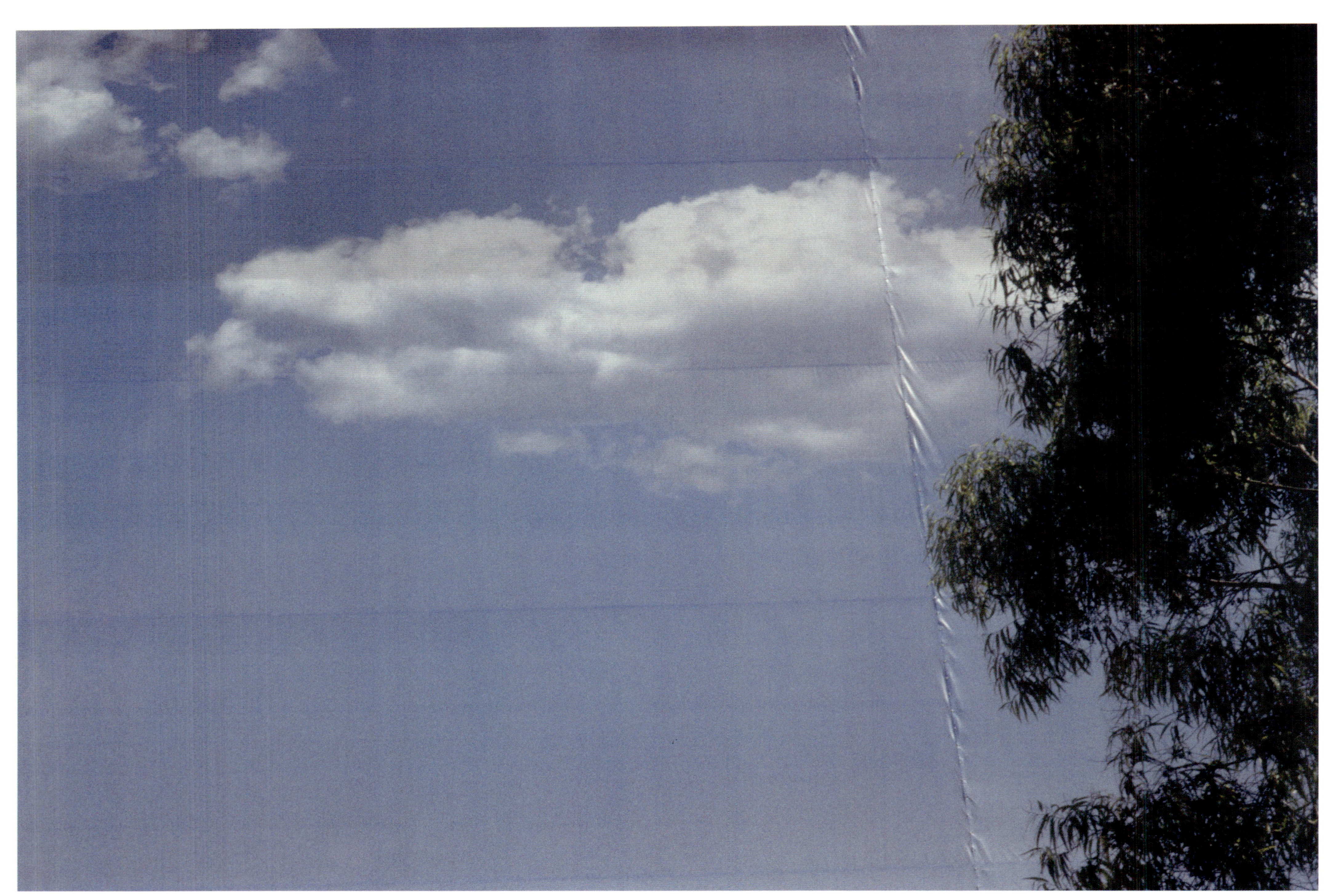

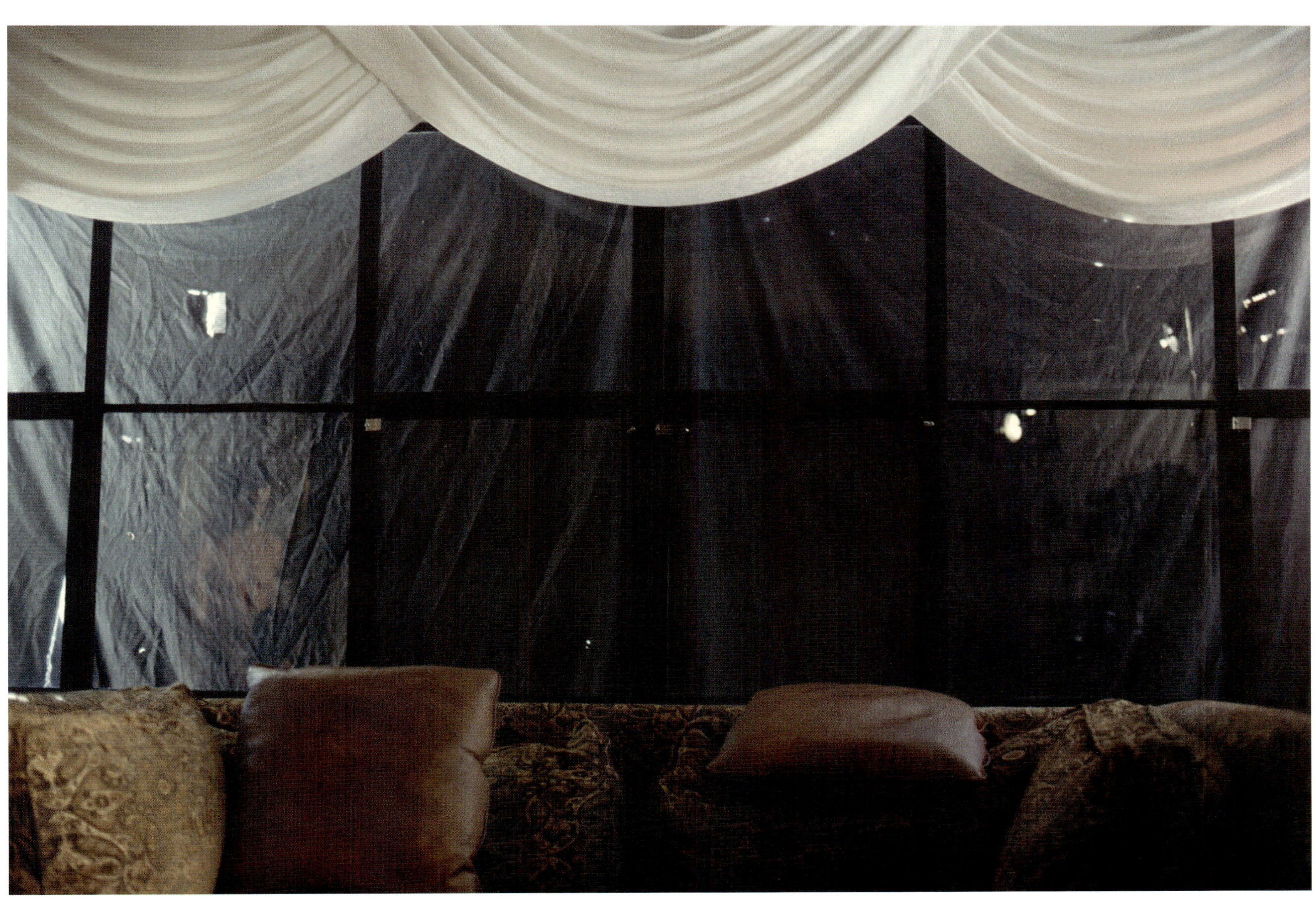

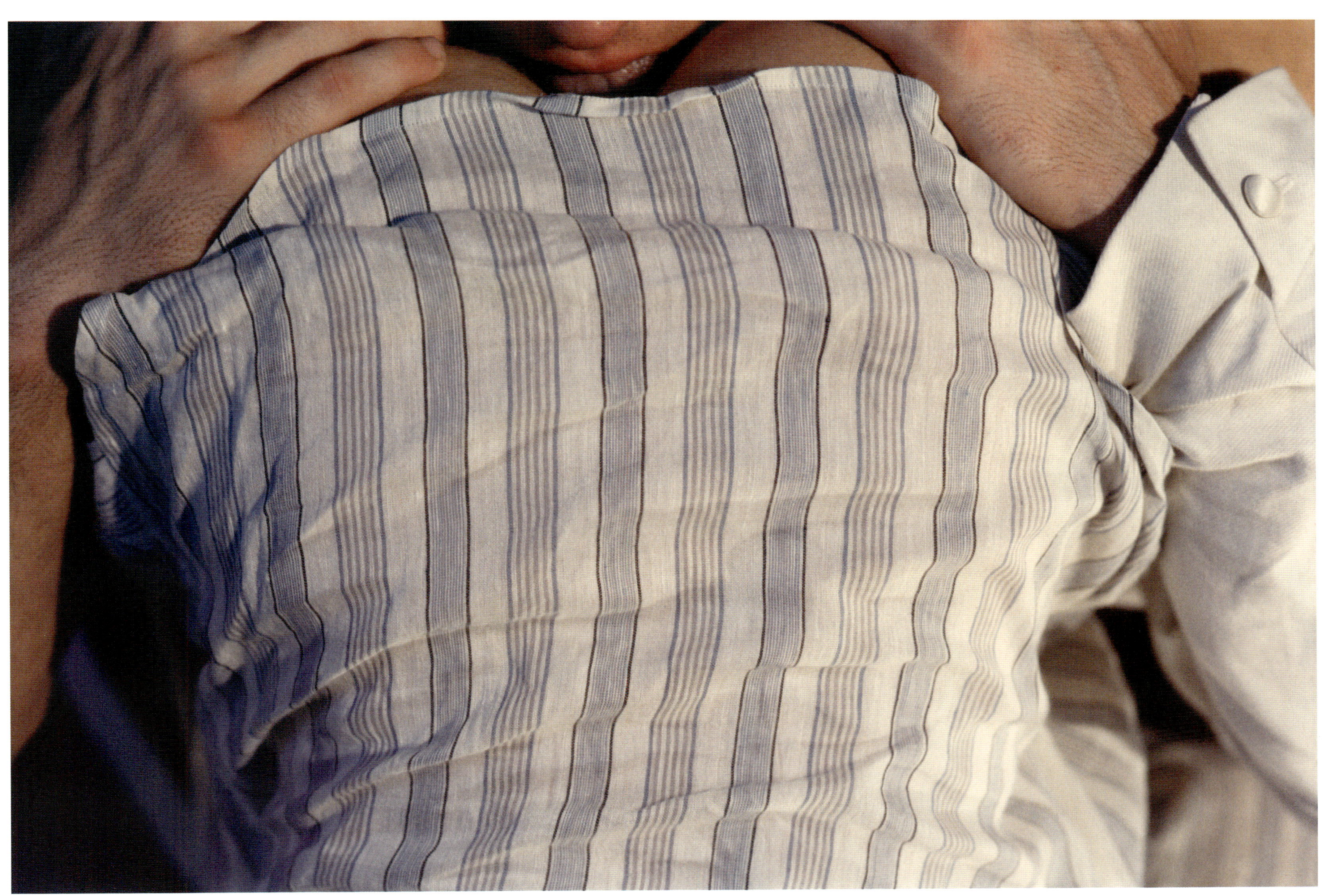

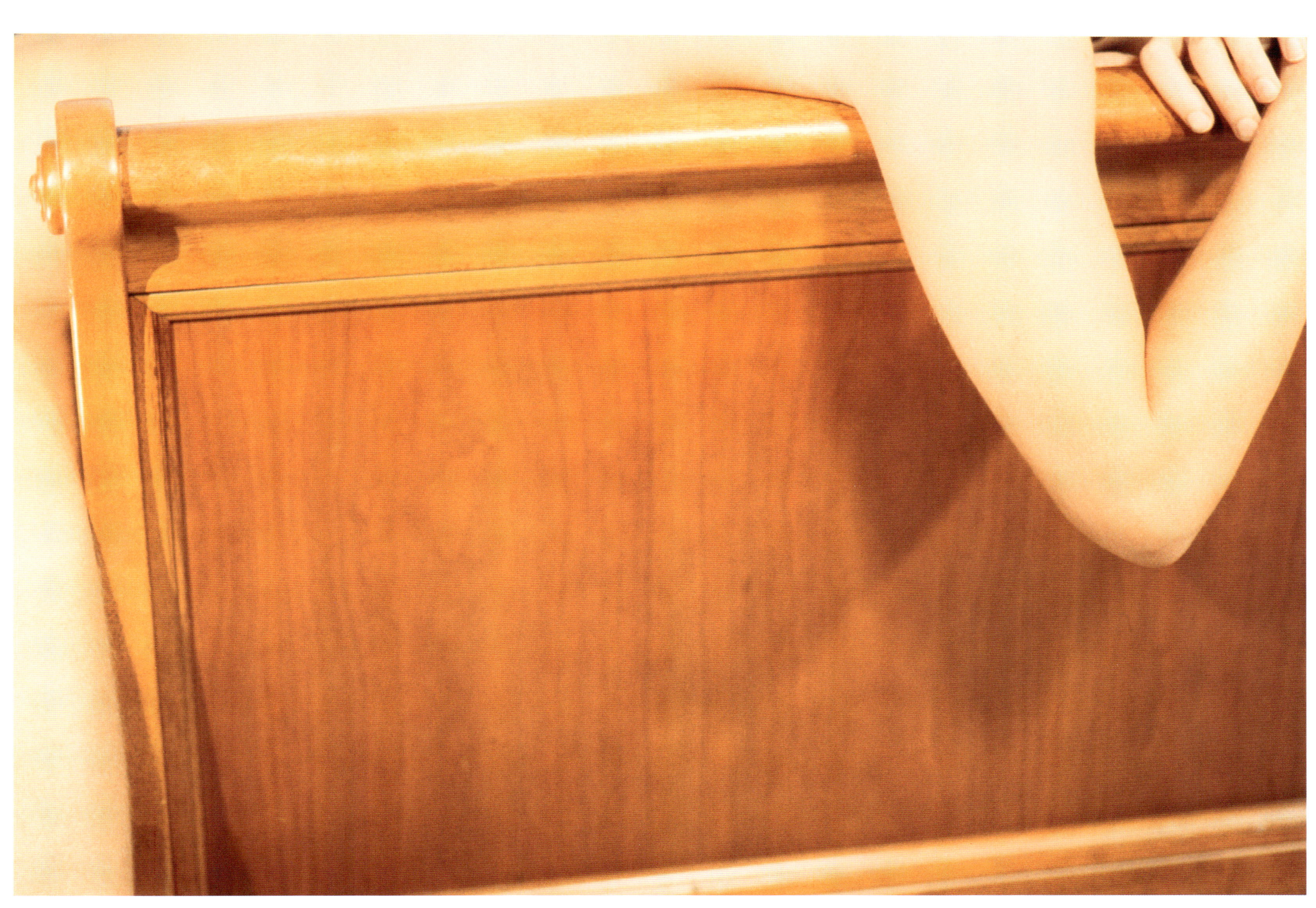

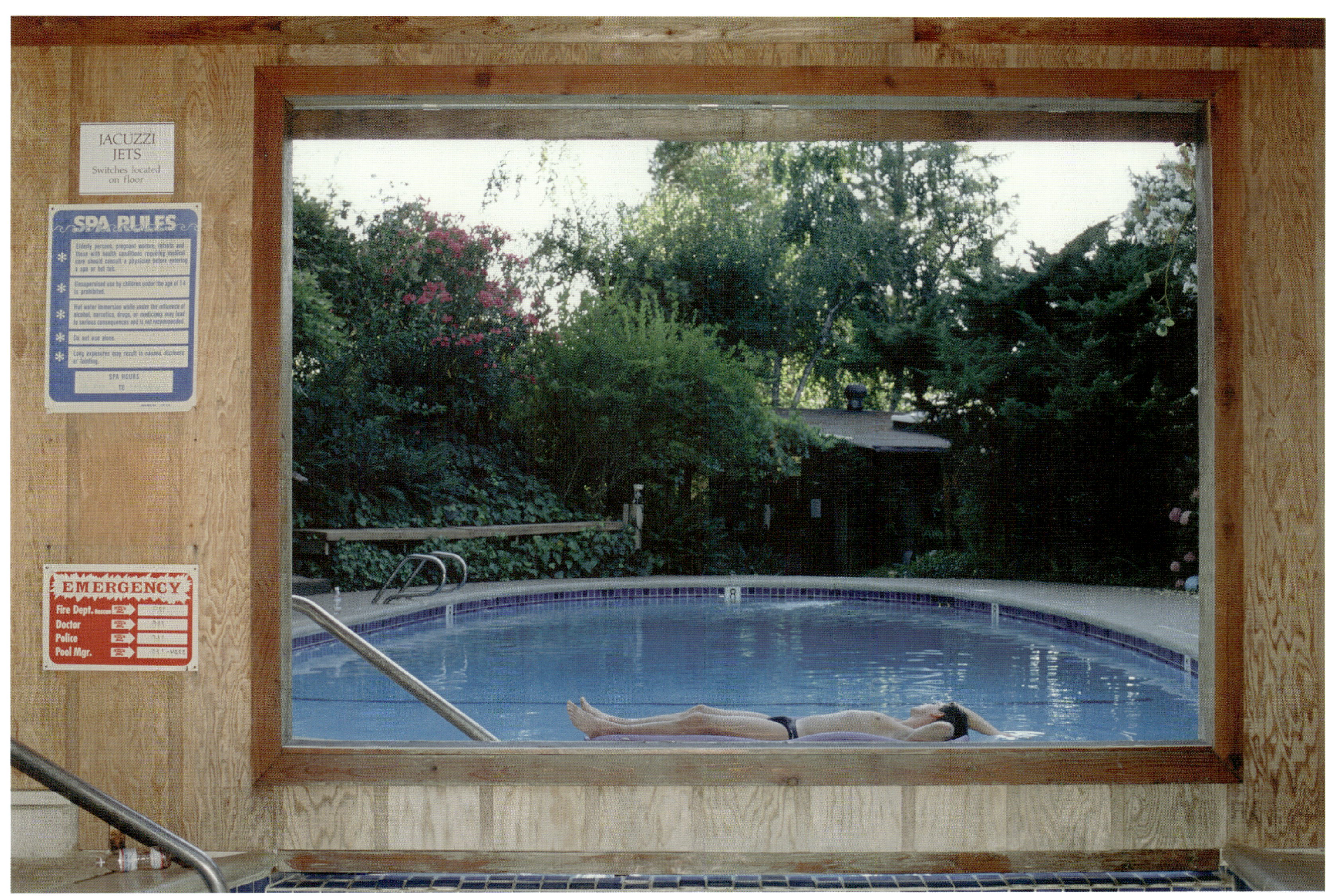
JACUZZI
JETS
Switches located
on floor

SPA RULES
* Elderly persons, pregnant women, infants and those with health conditions requiring medical care should consult a physician before entering a spa or hot tub.
* Unsupervised use by children under the age of 14 is prohibited.
* Hot water immersion while under the influence of alcohol, narcotics, drugs, or medicines may lead to serious consequences and is not recommended.
* Do not use alone.
* Long exposures may result in nausea, dizziness or fainting.
SPA HOURS
TO

EMERGENCY
Fire Dept. Rescue 911
Doctor 911
Police 911
Pool Mgr. 911-HERE

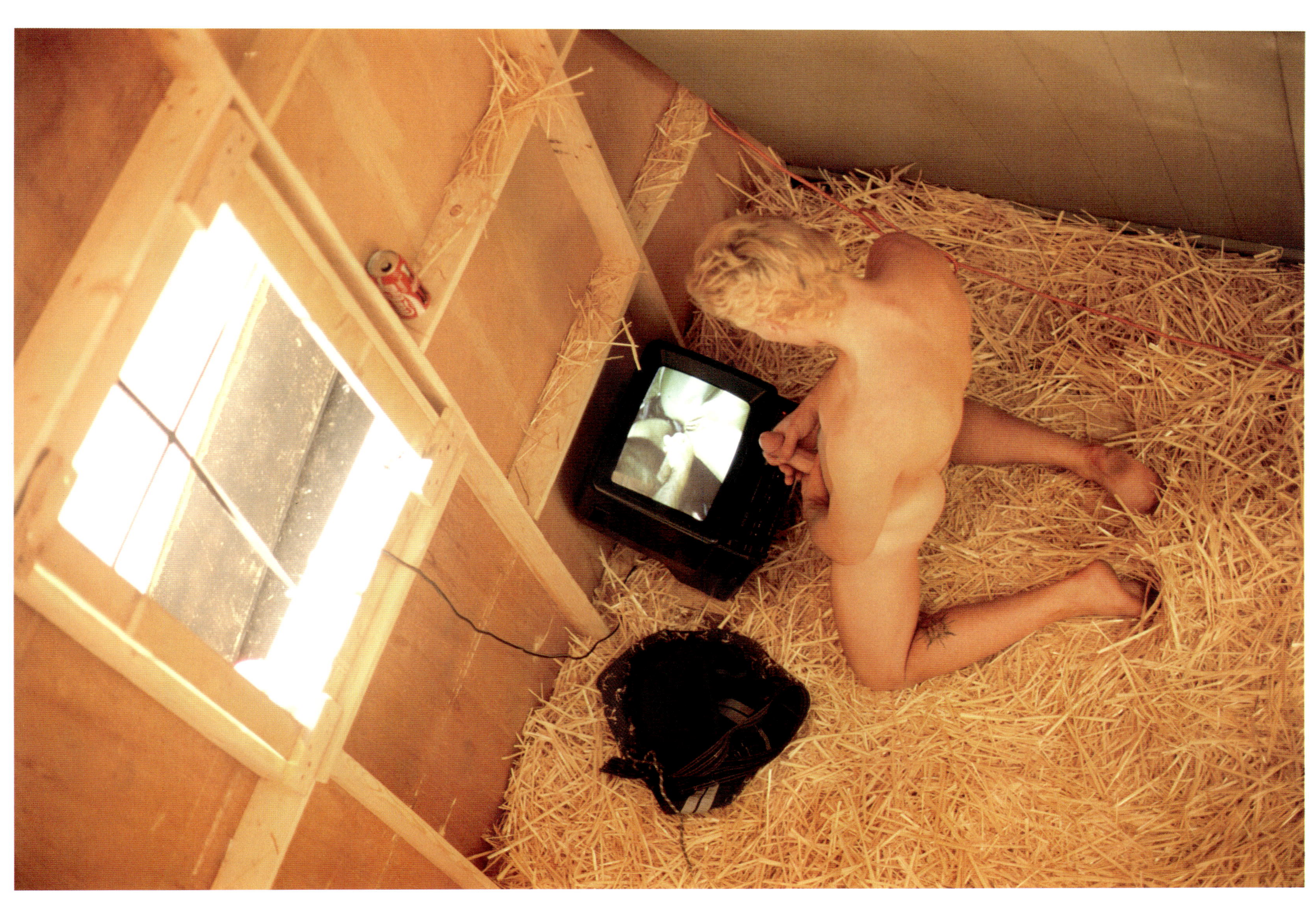

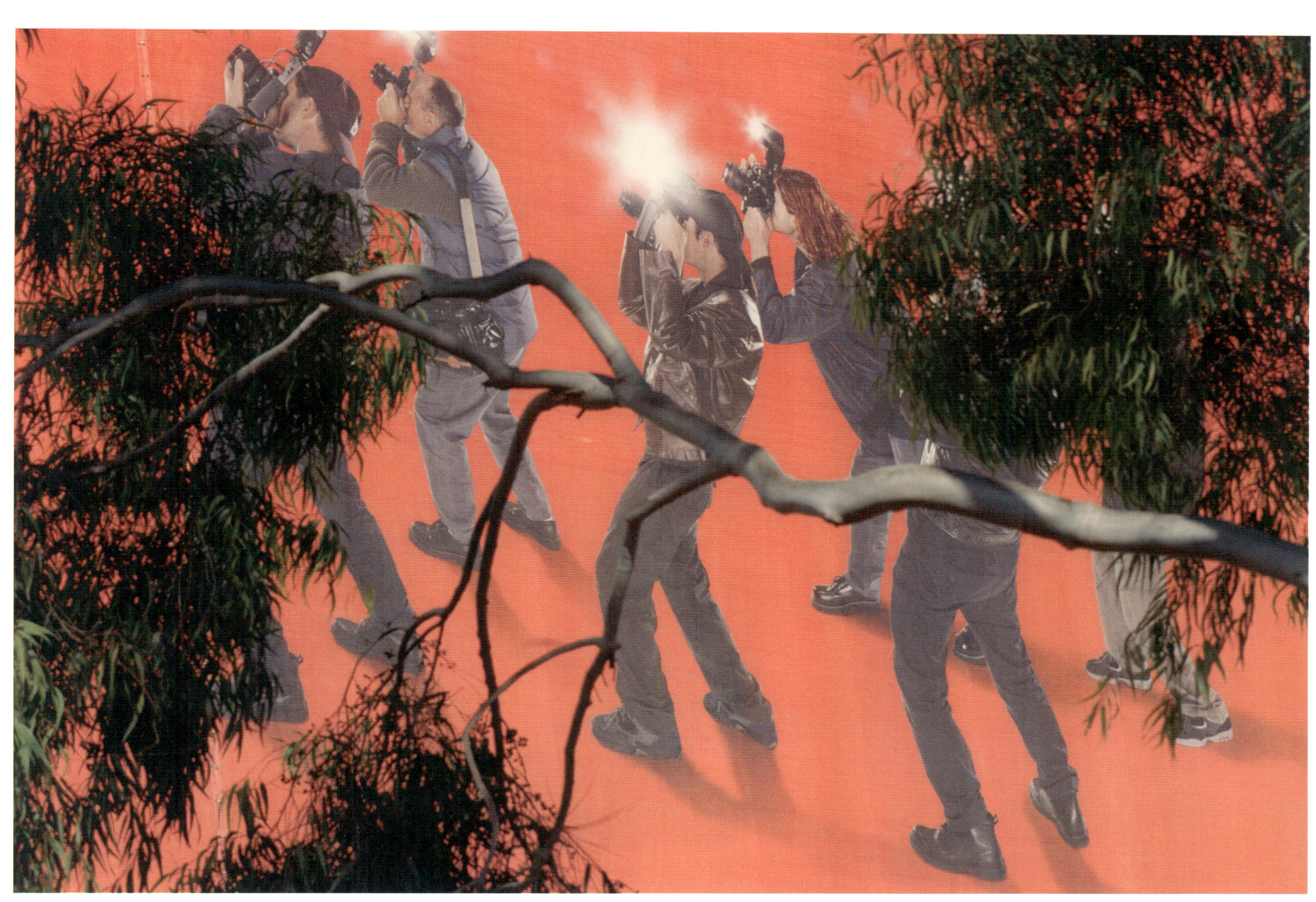

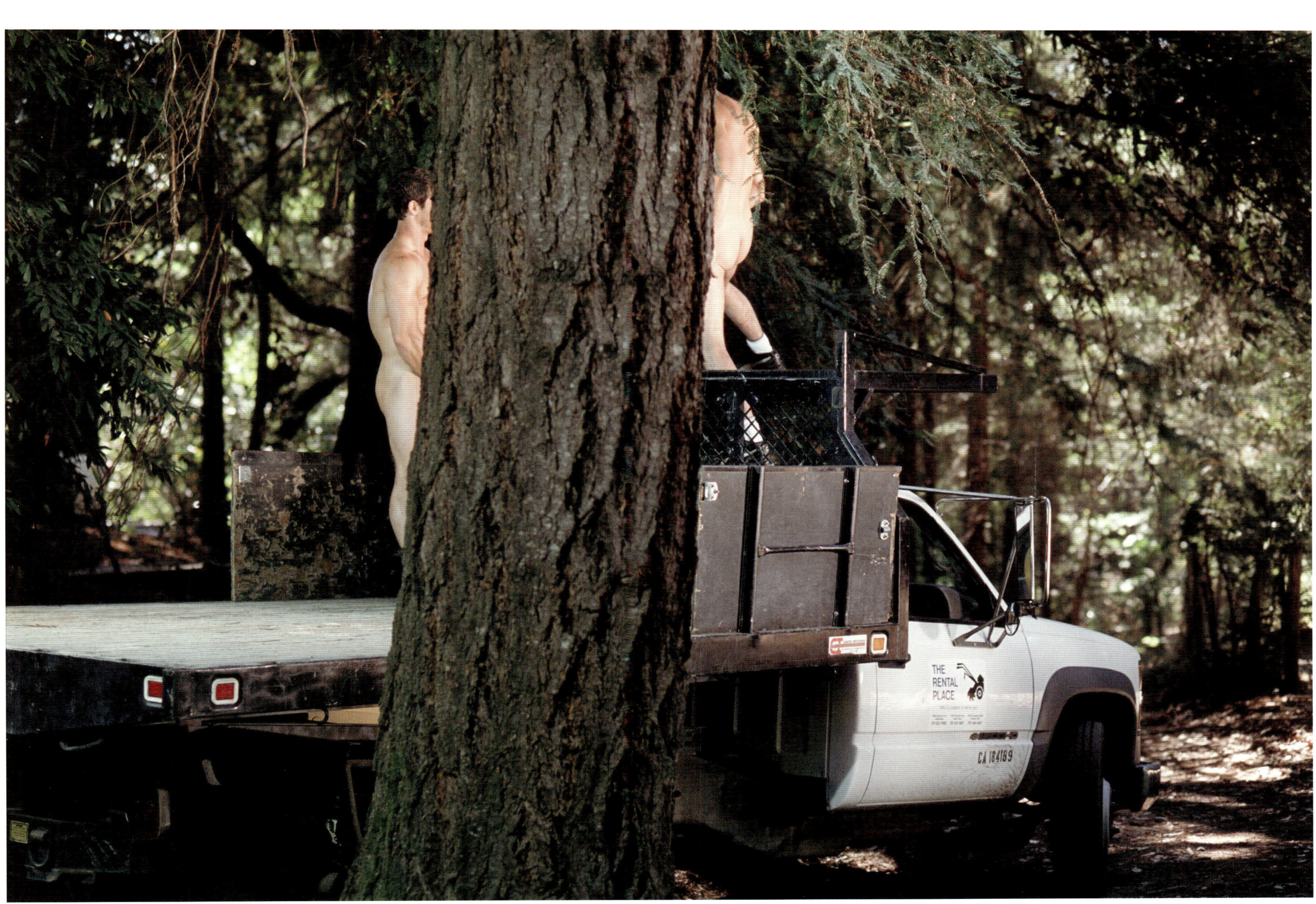

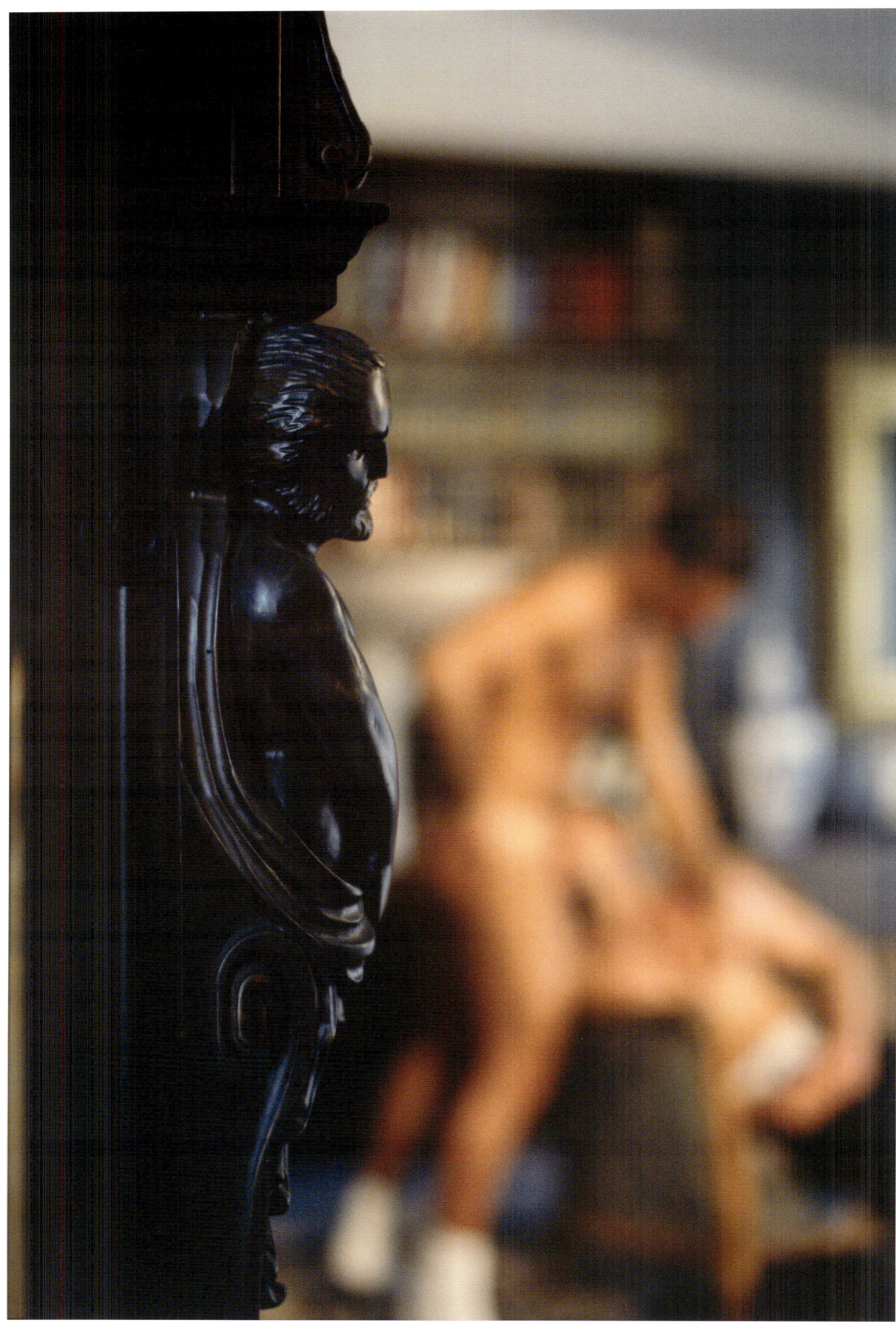

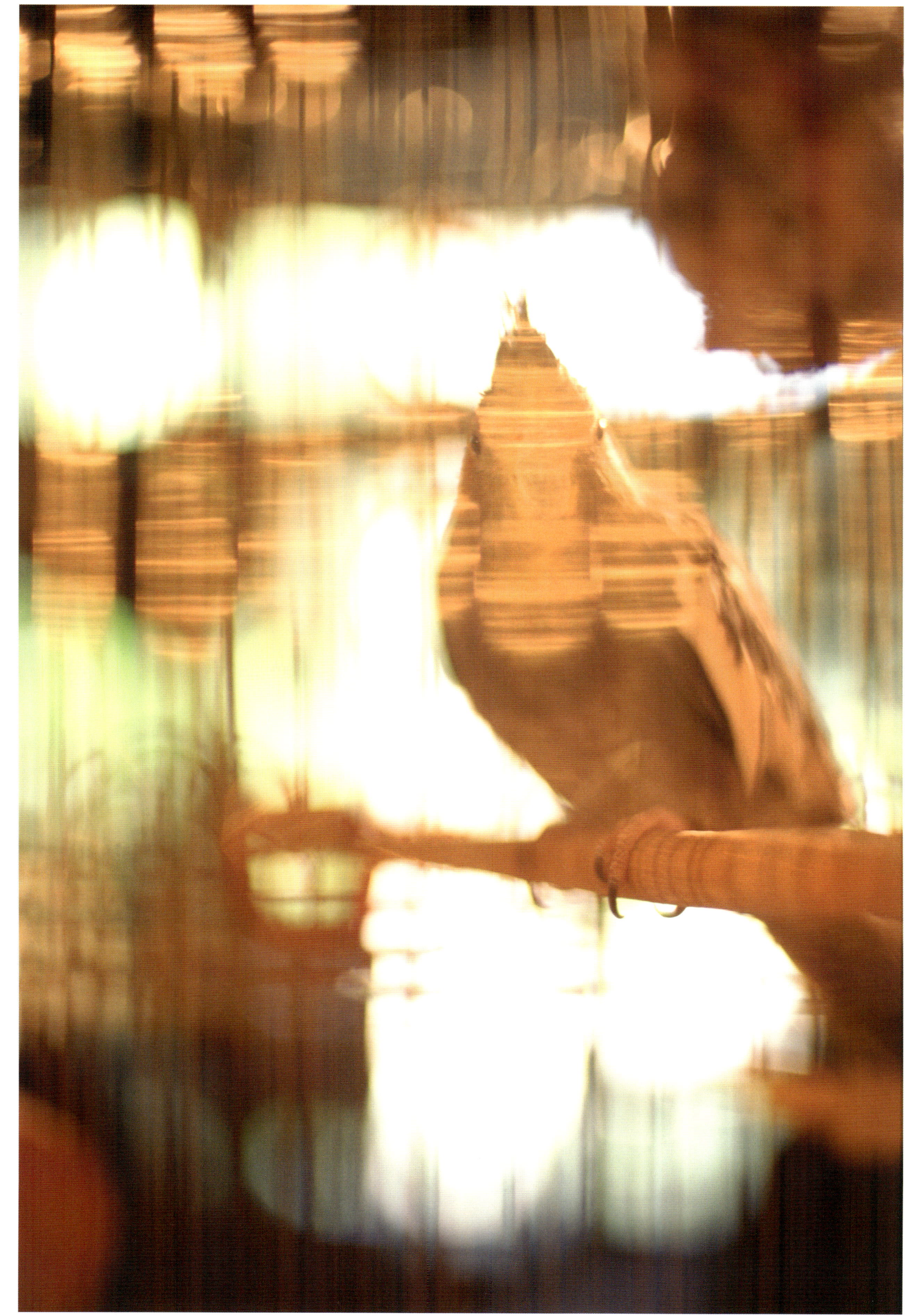

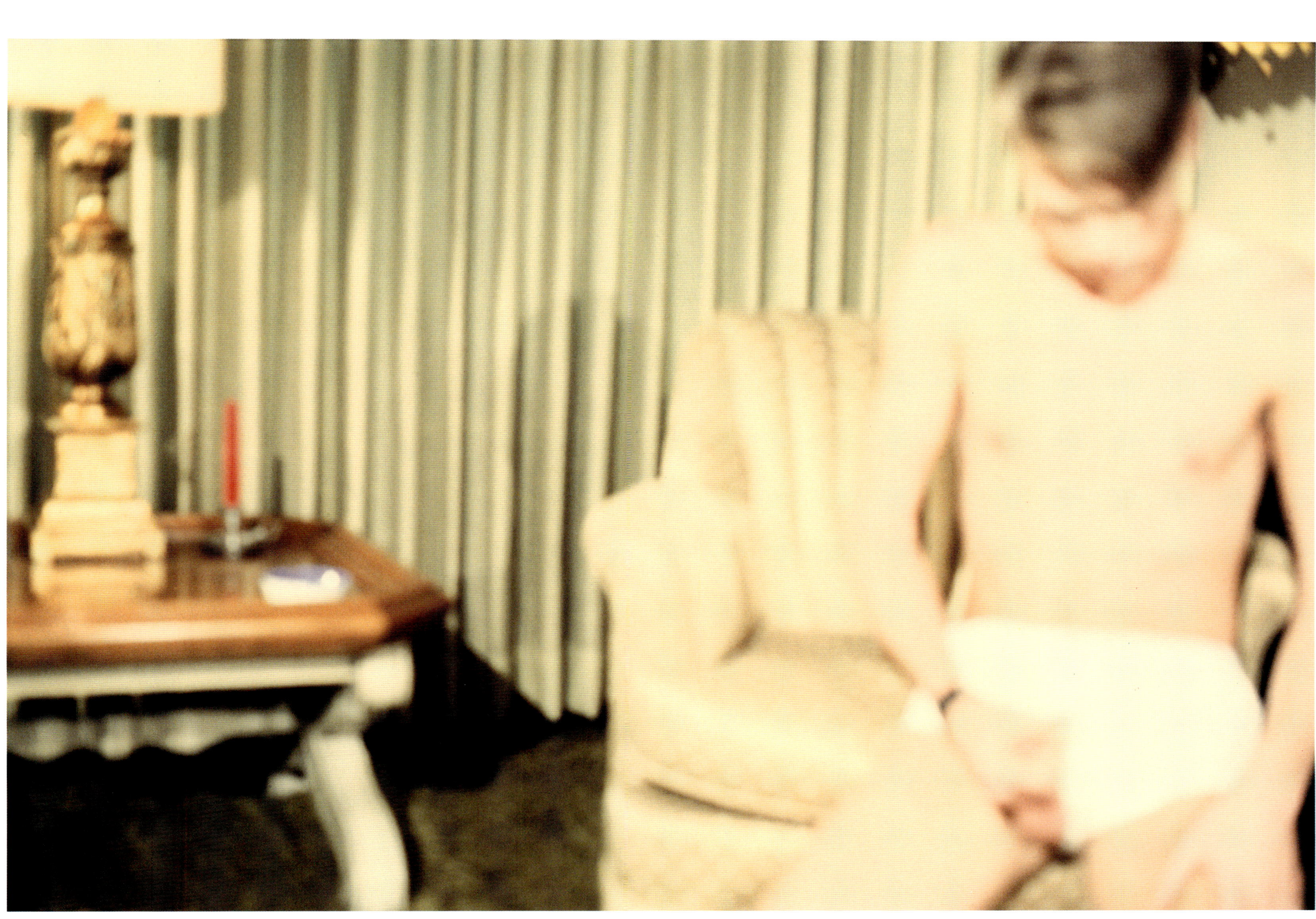

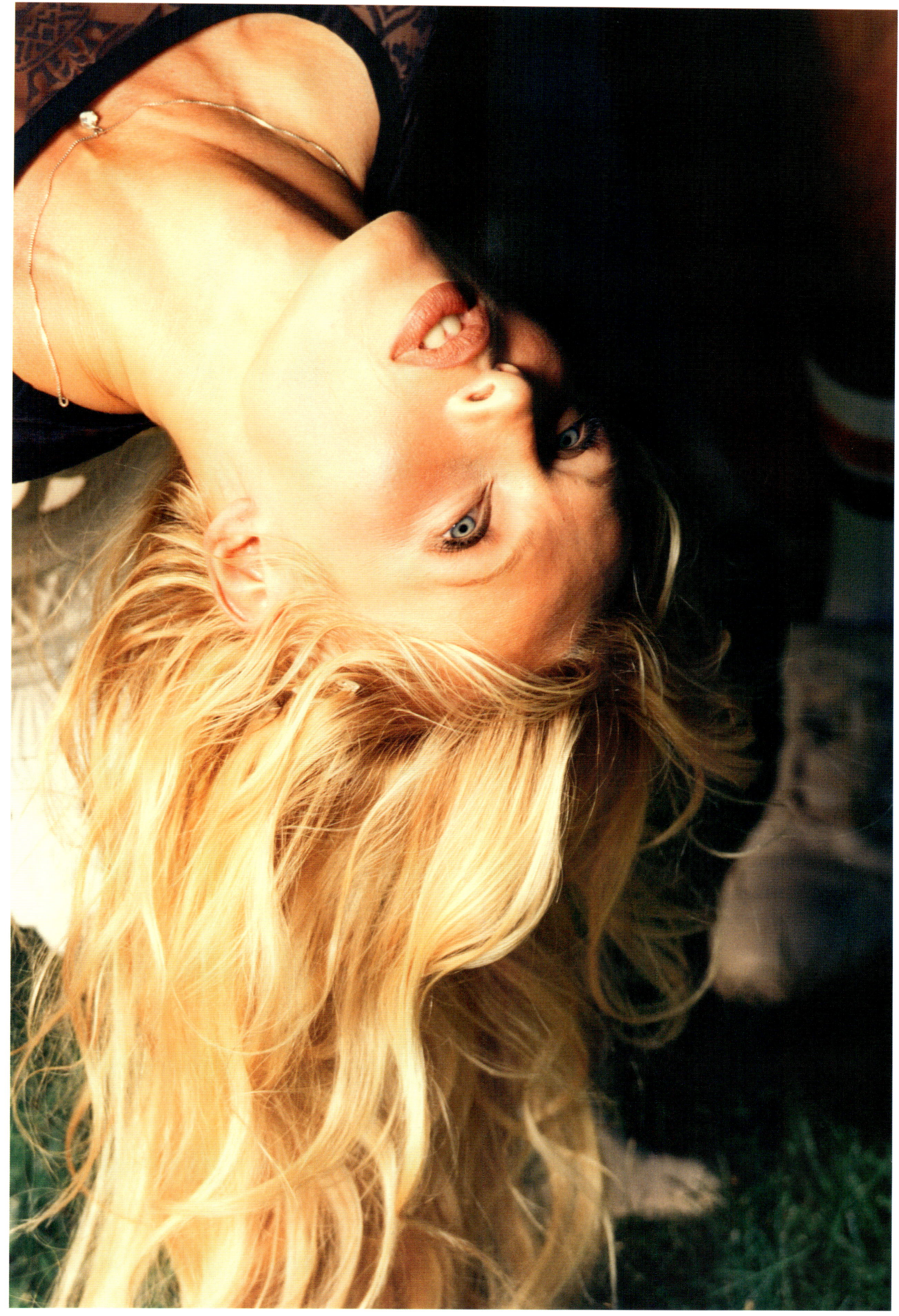

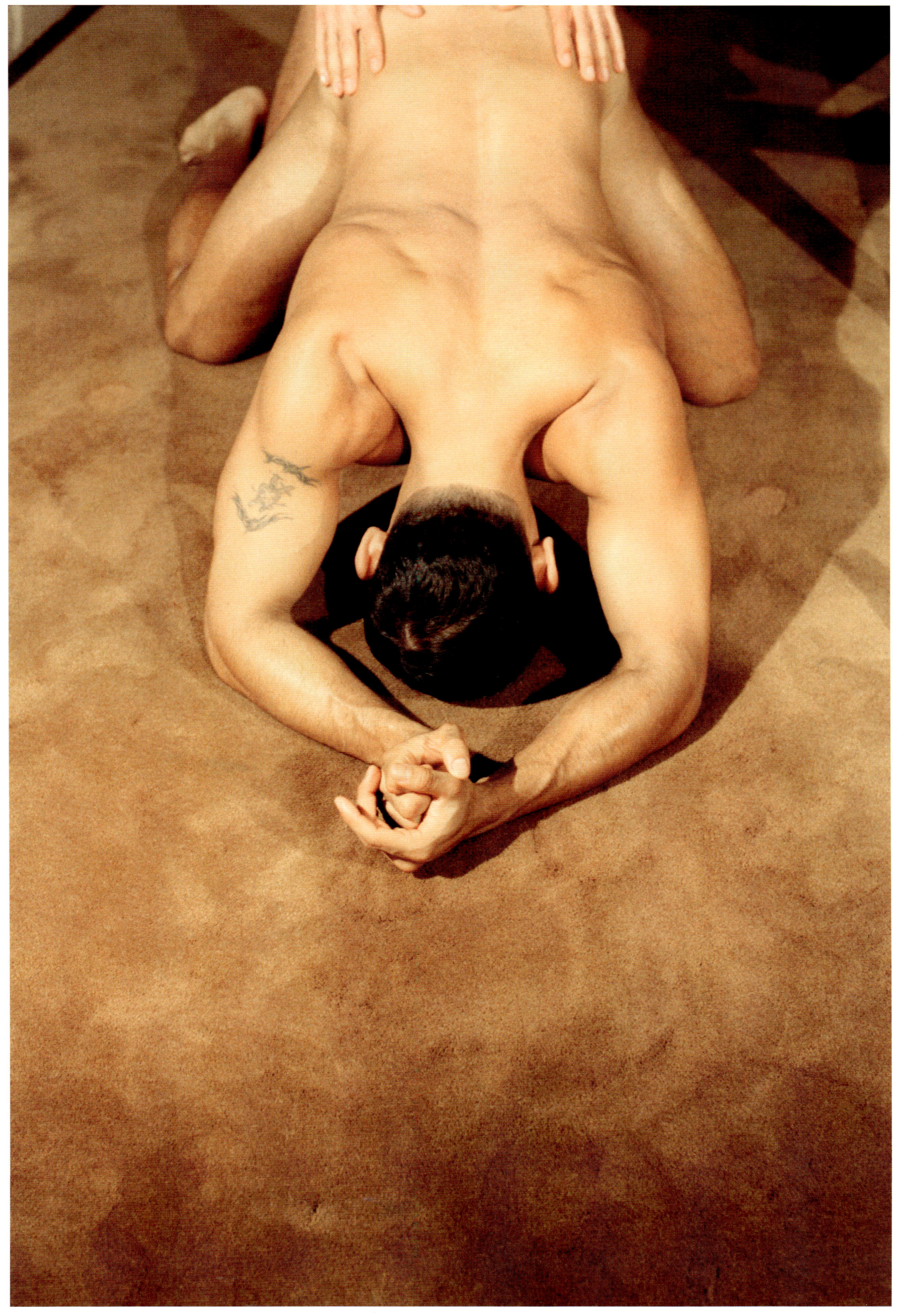

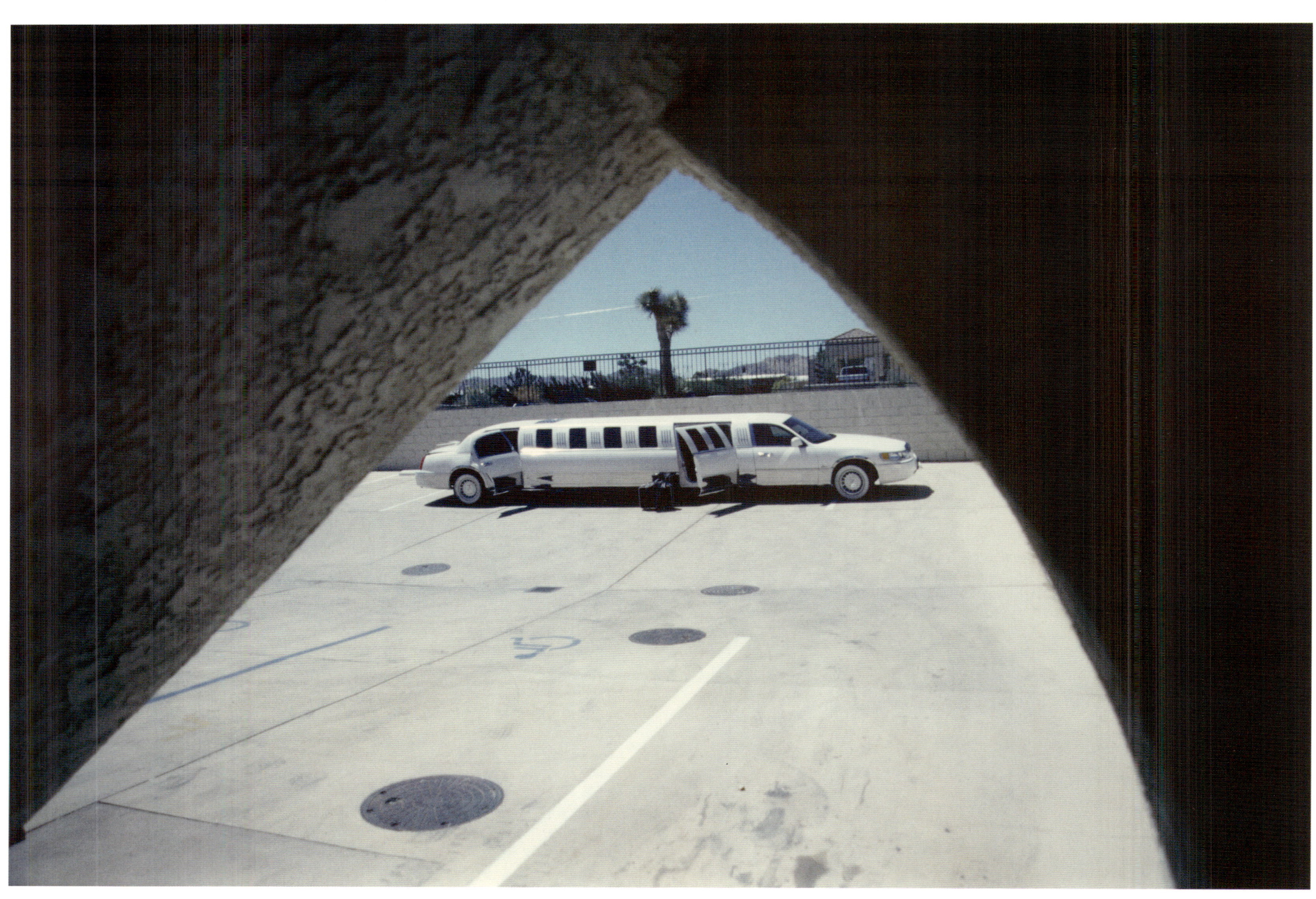

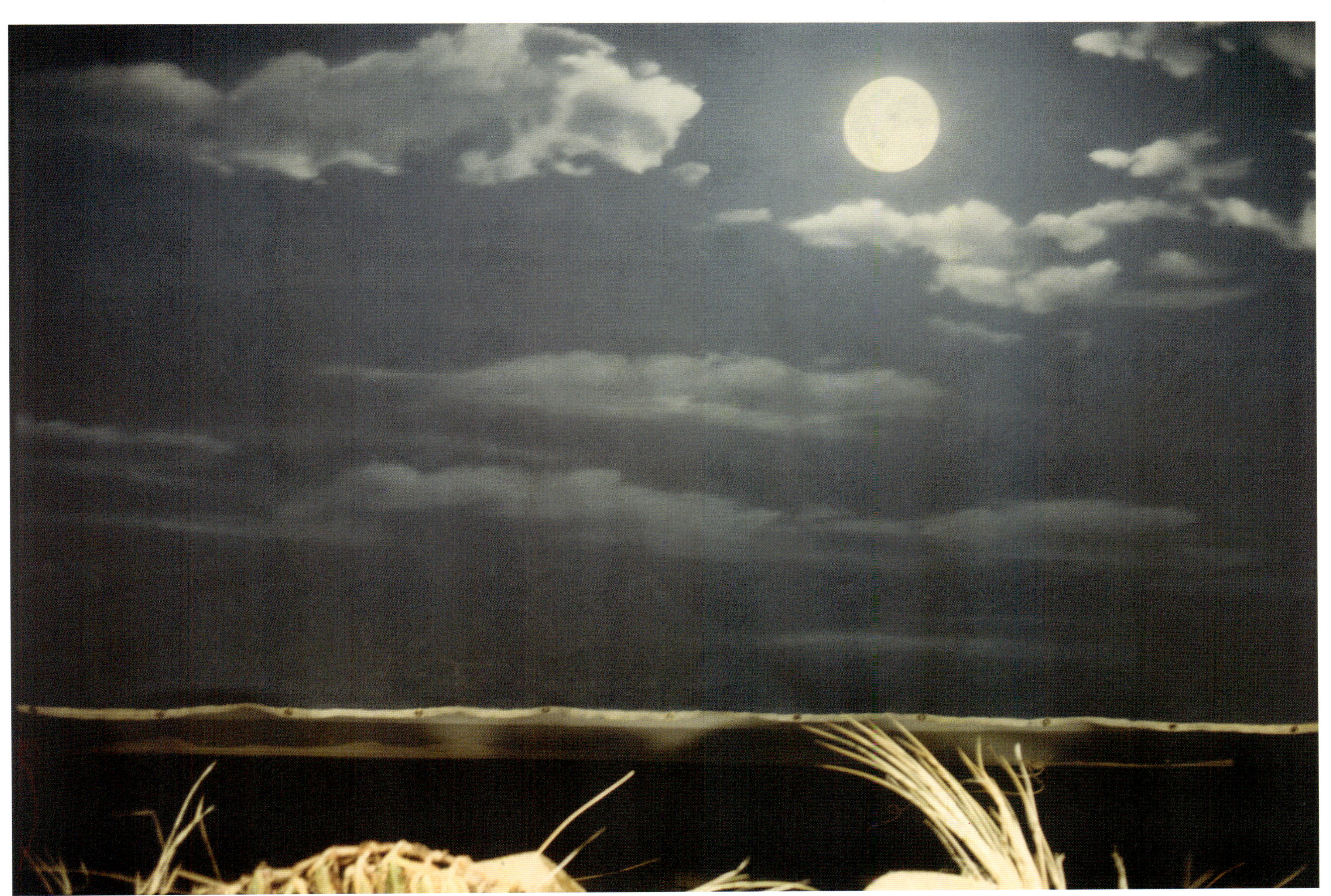

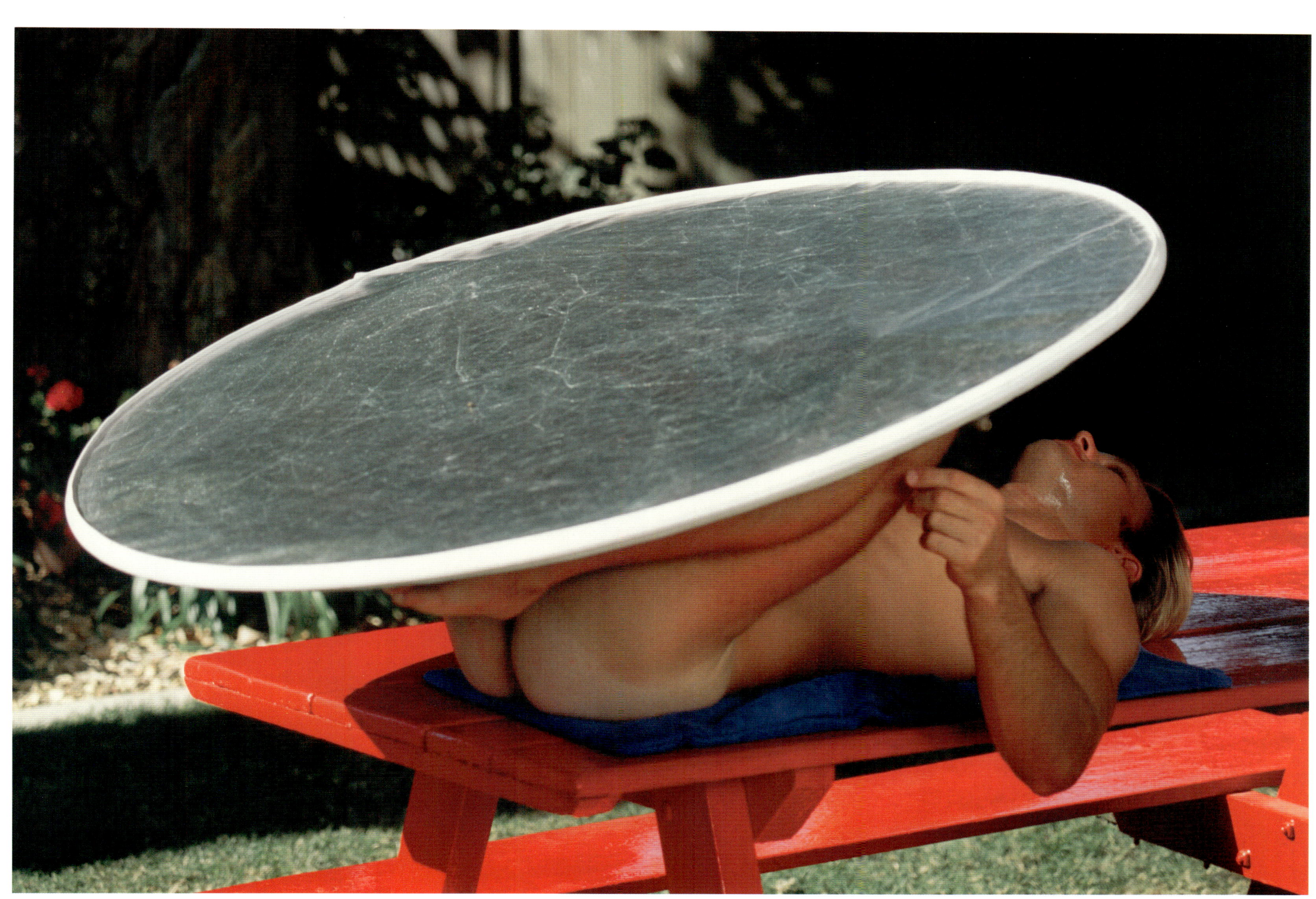

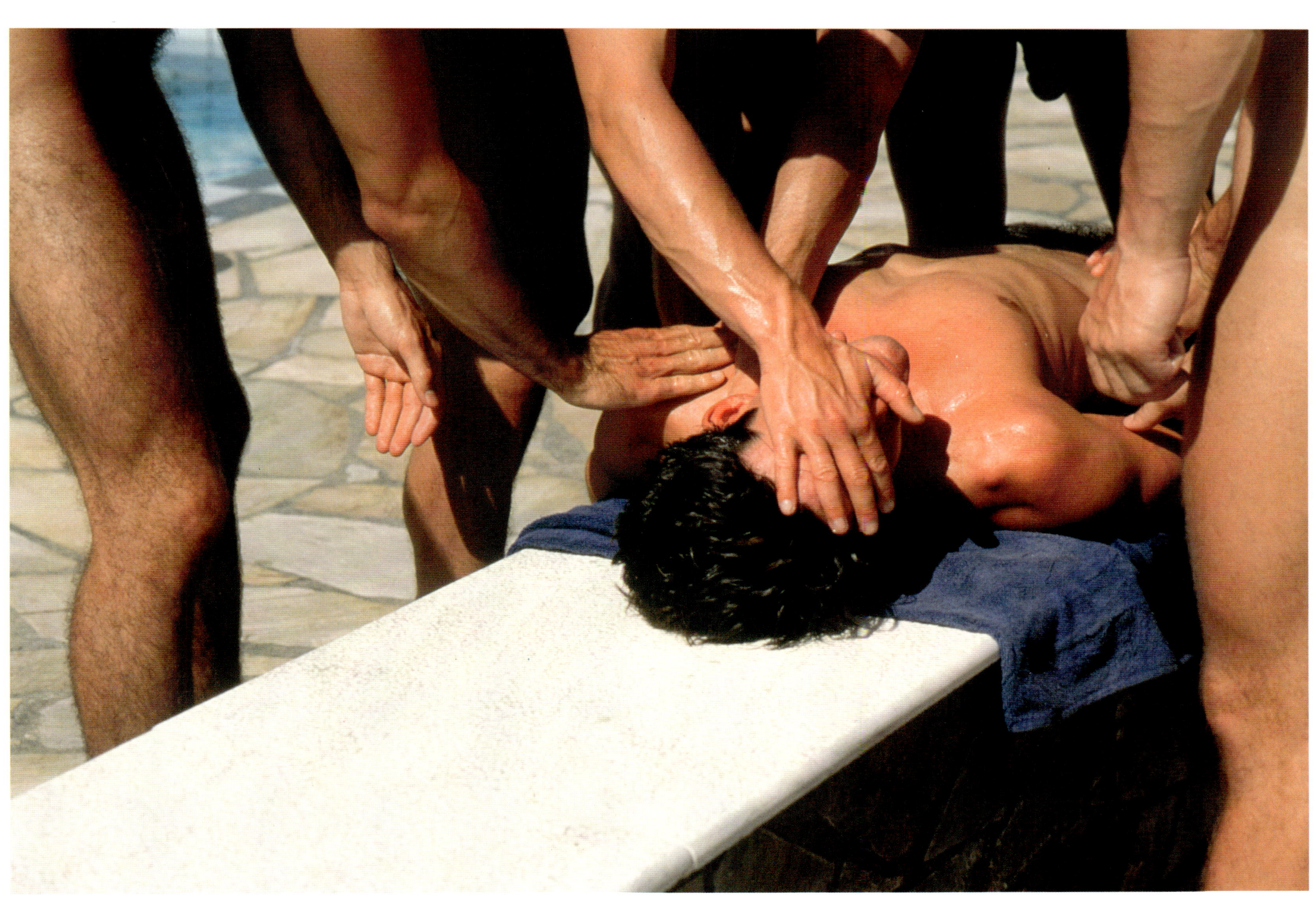

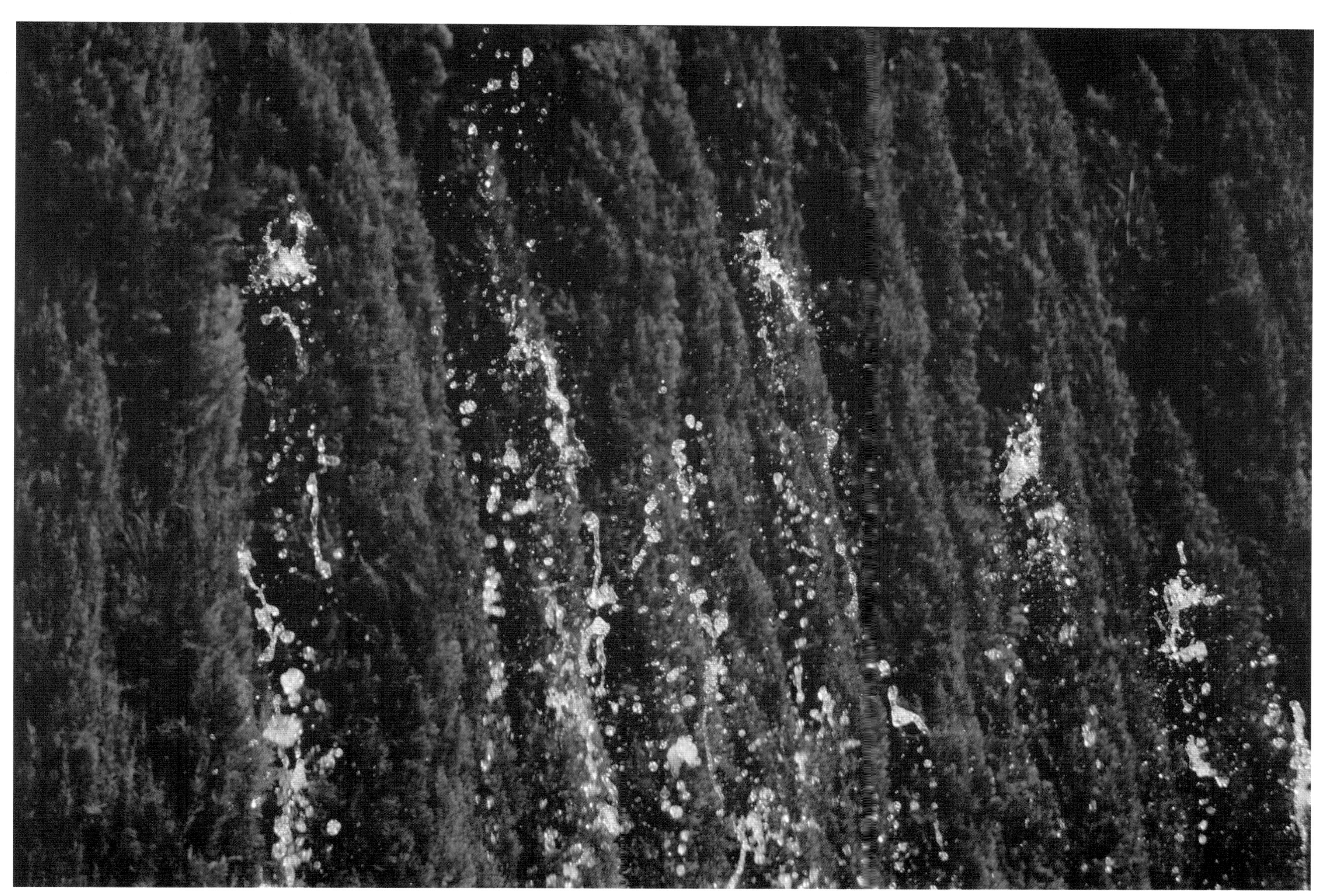

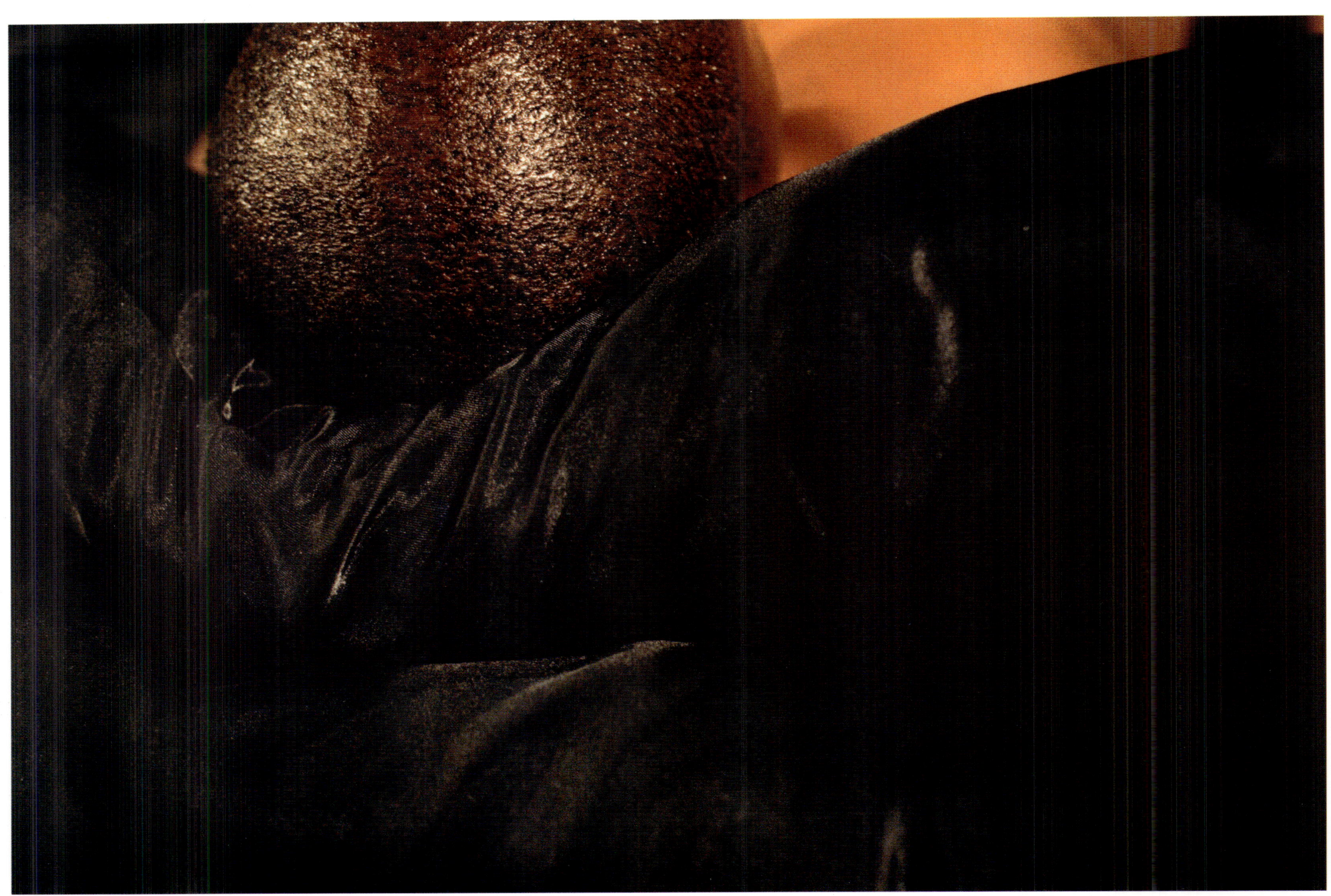

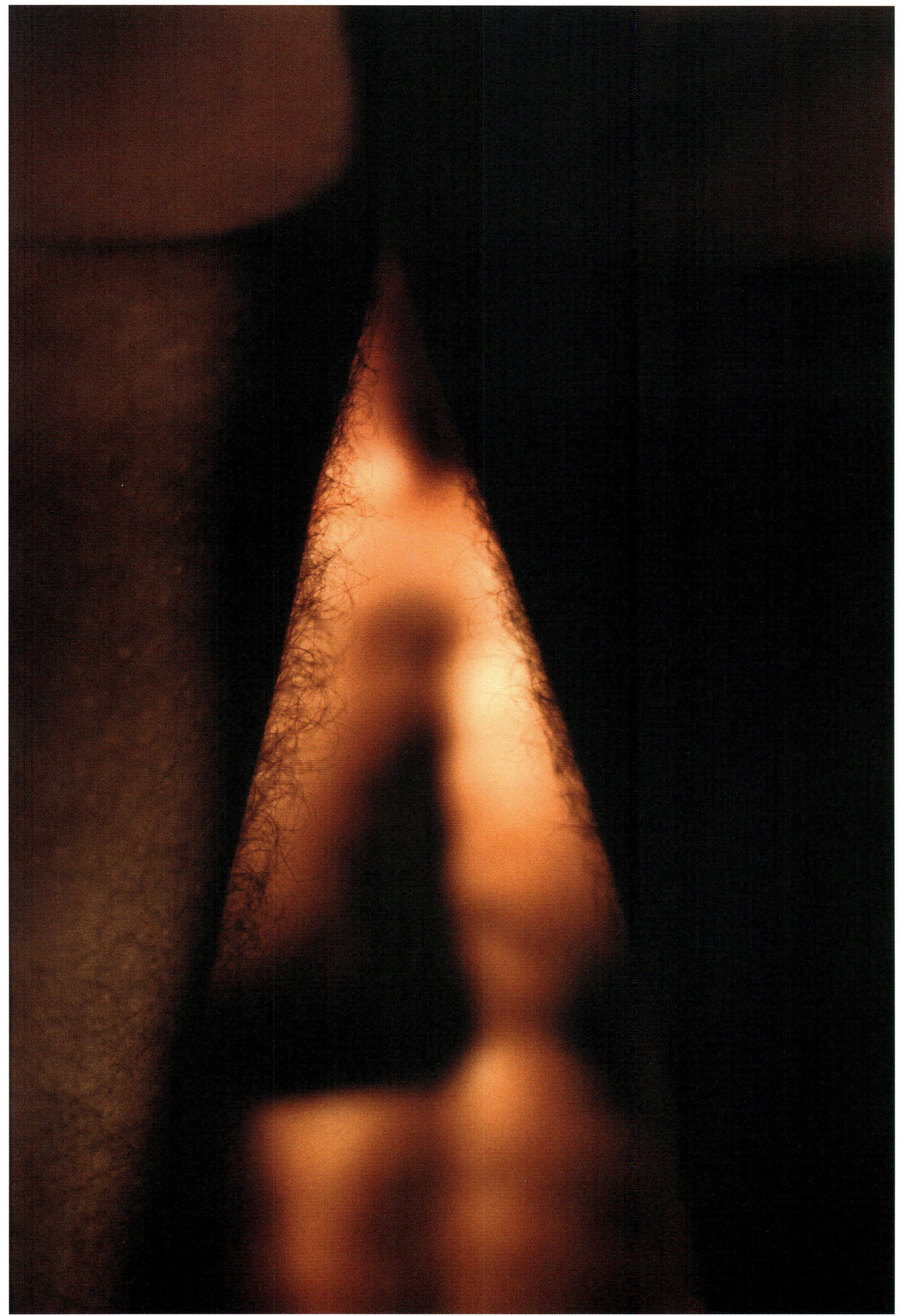

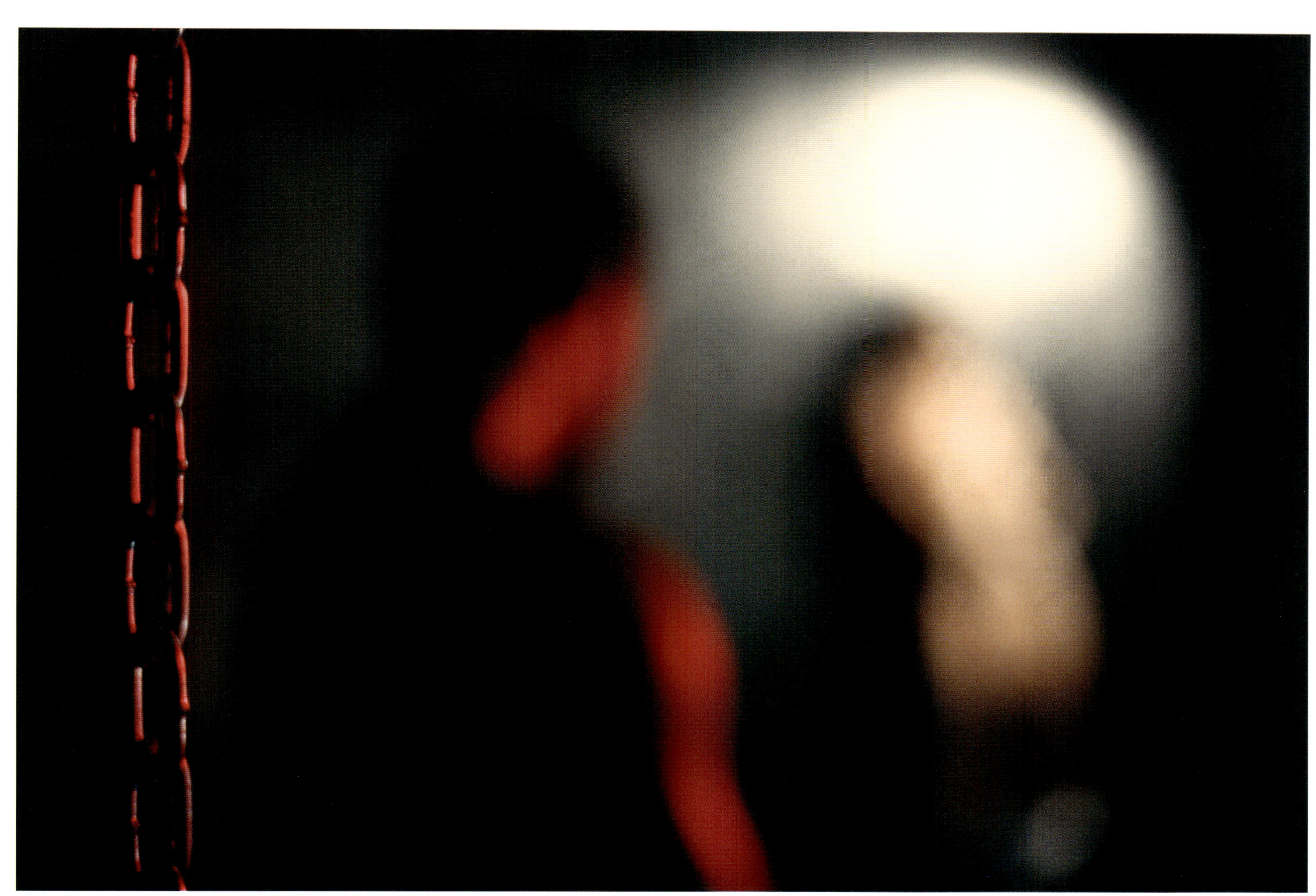

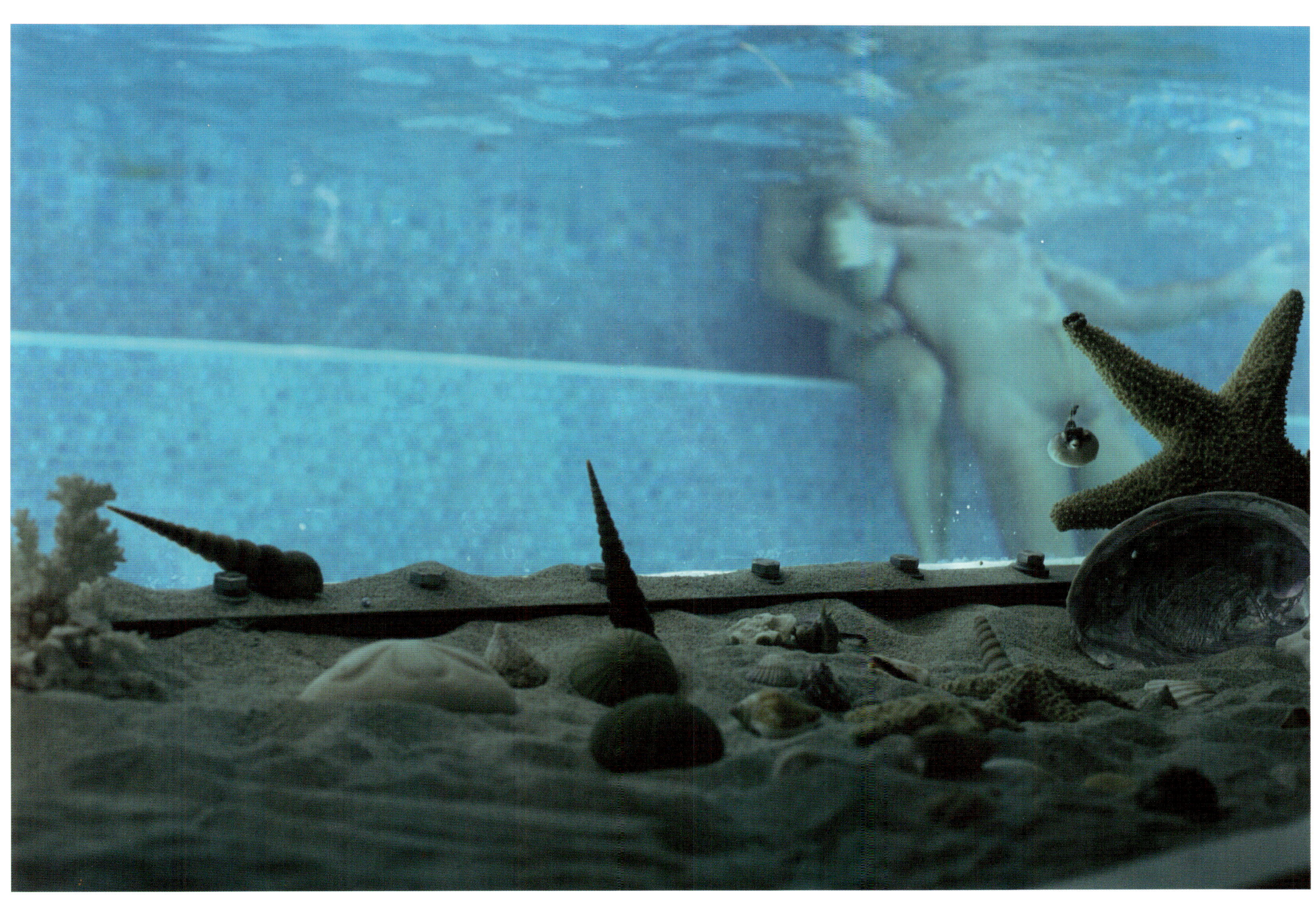

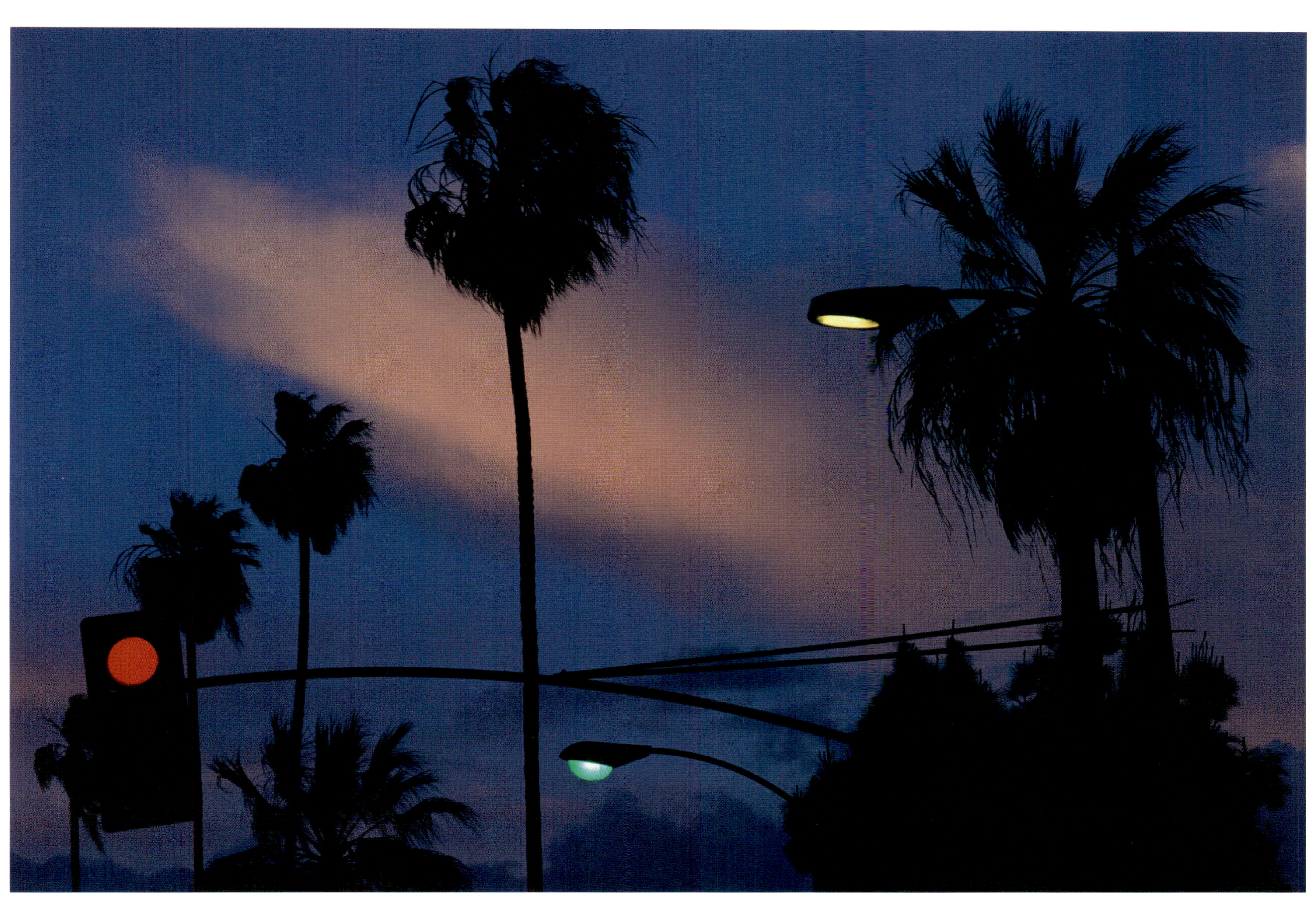

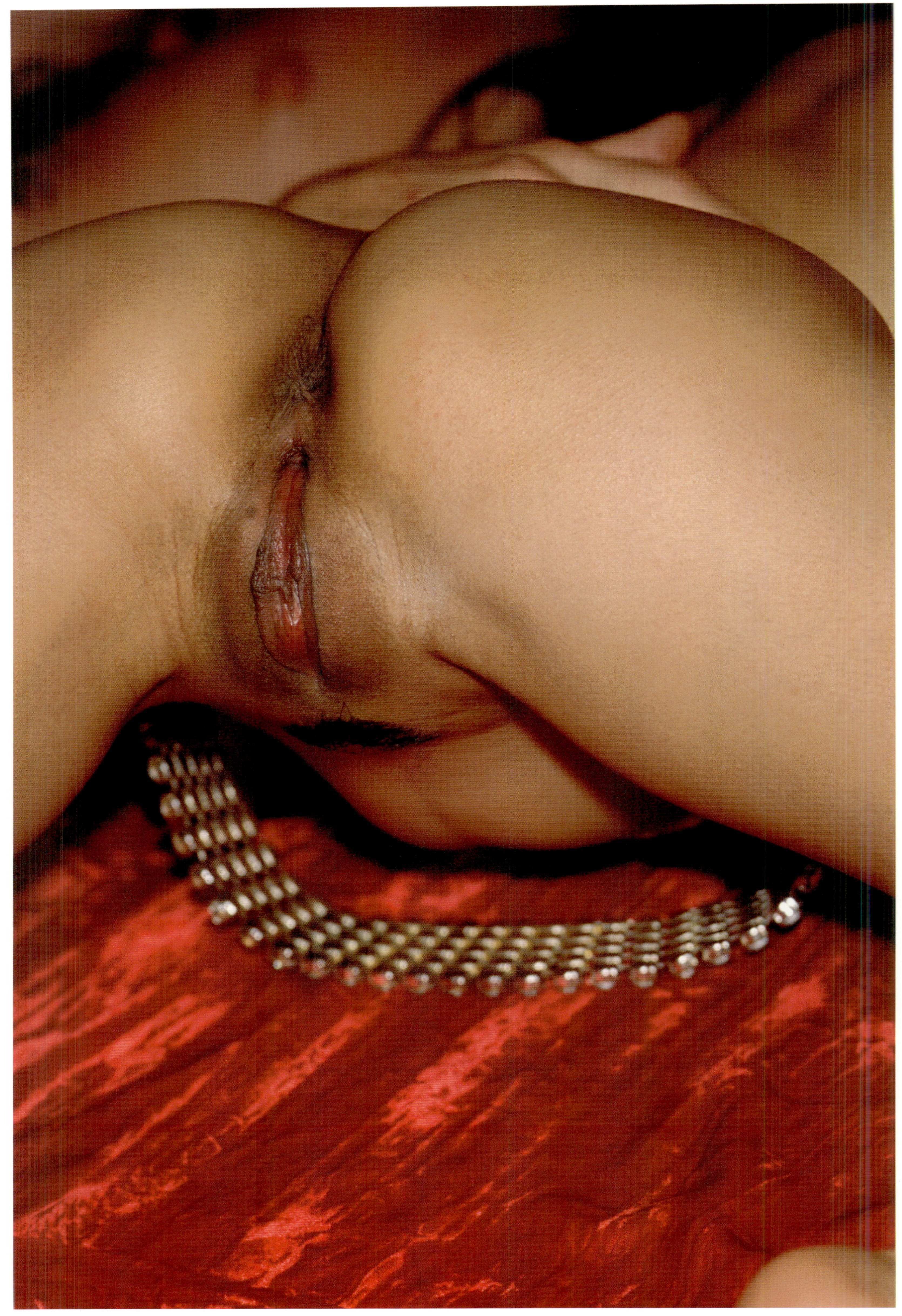

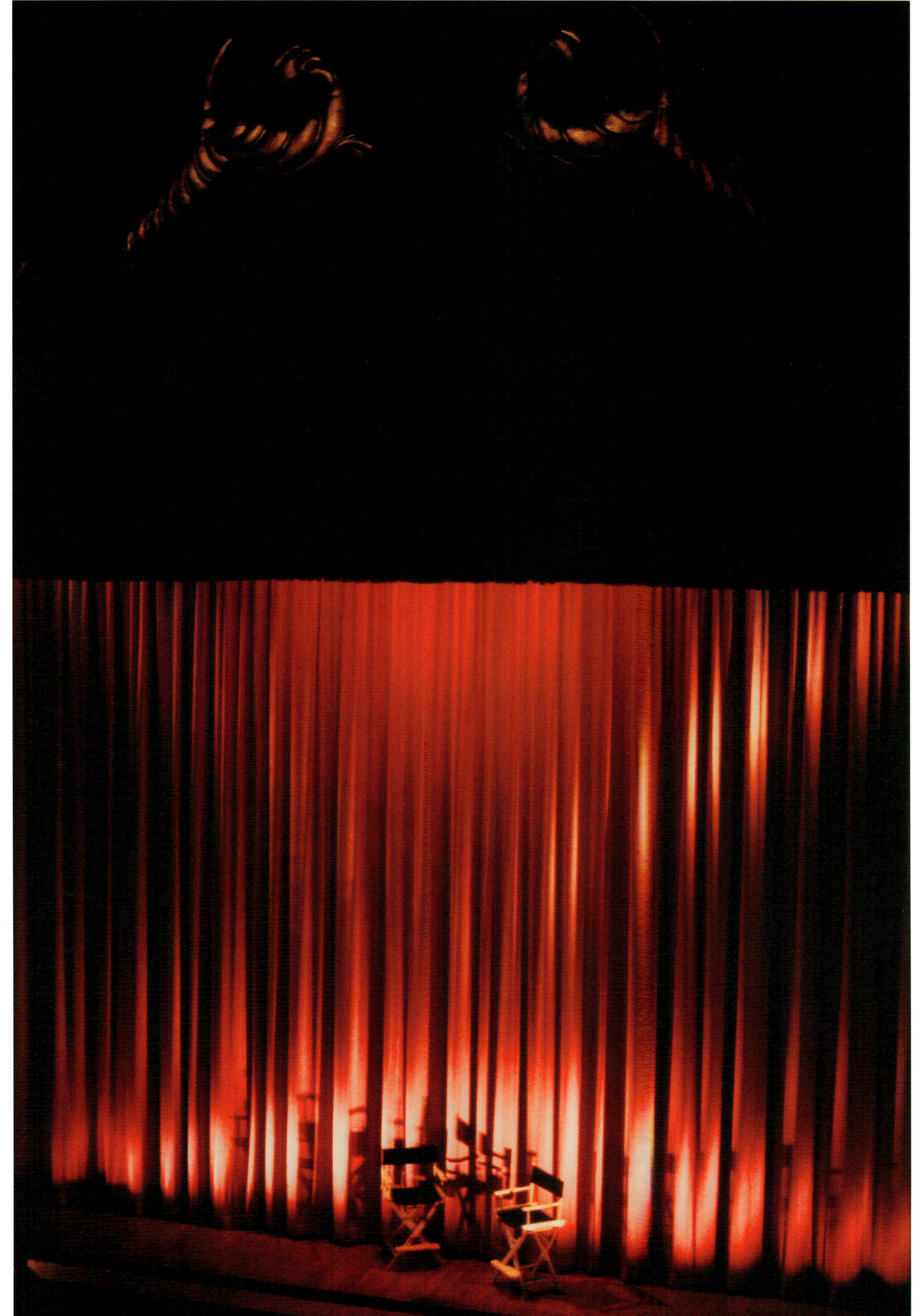

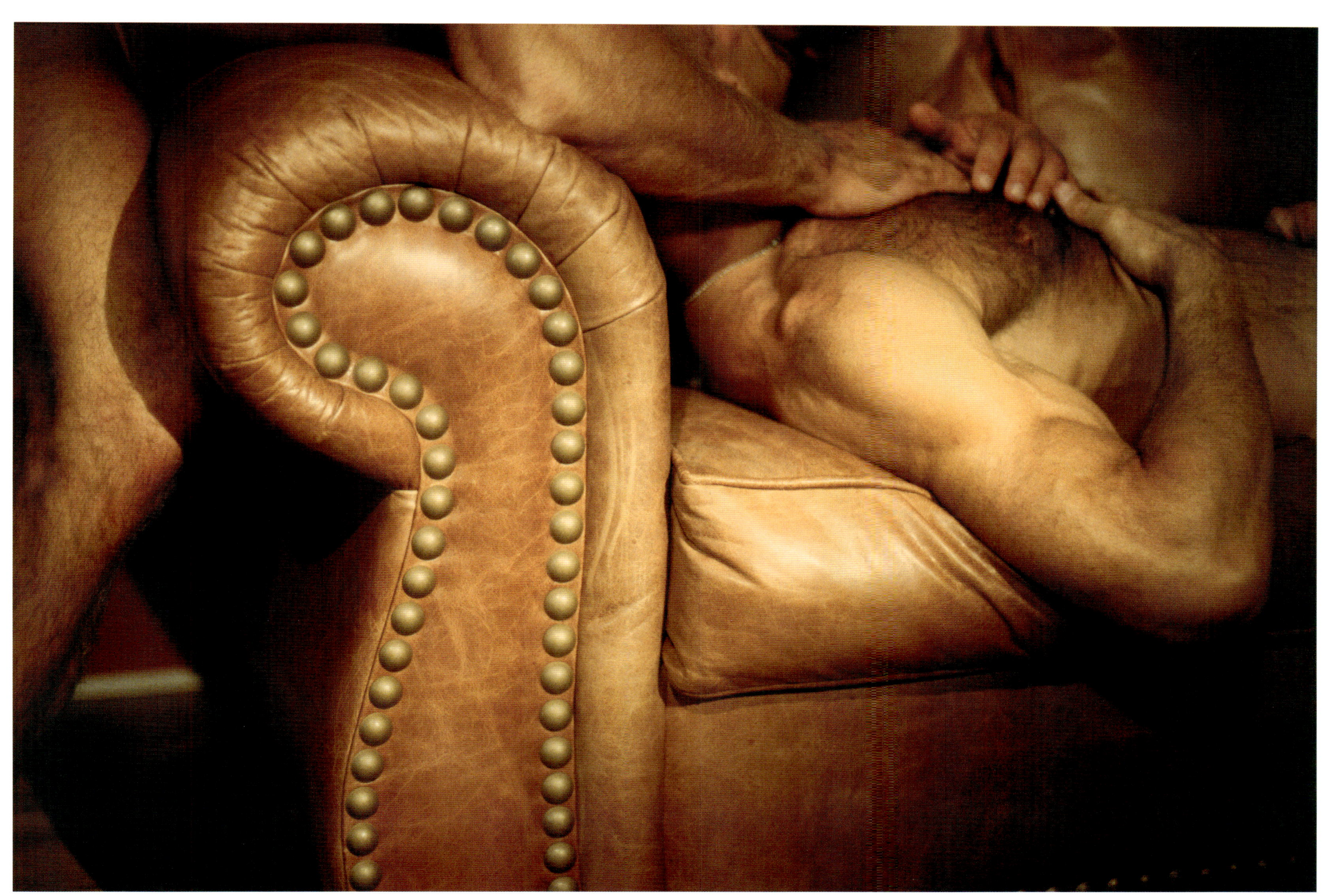

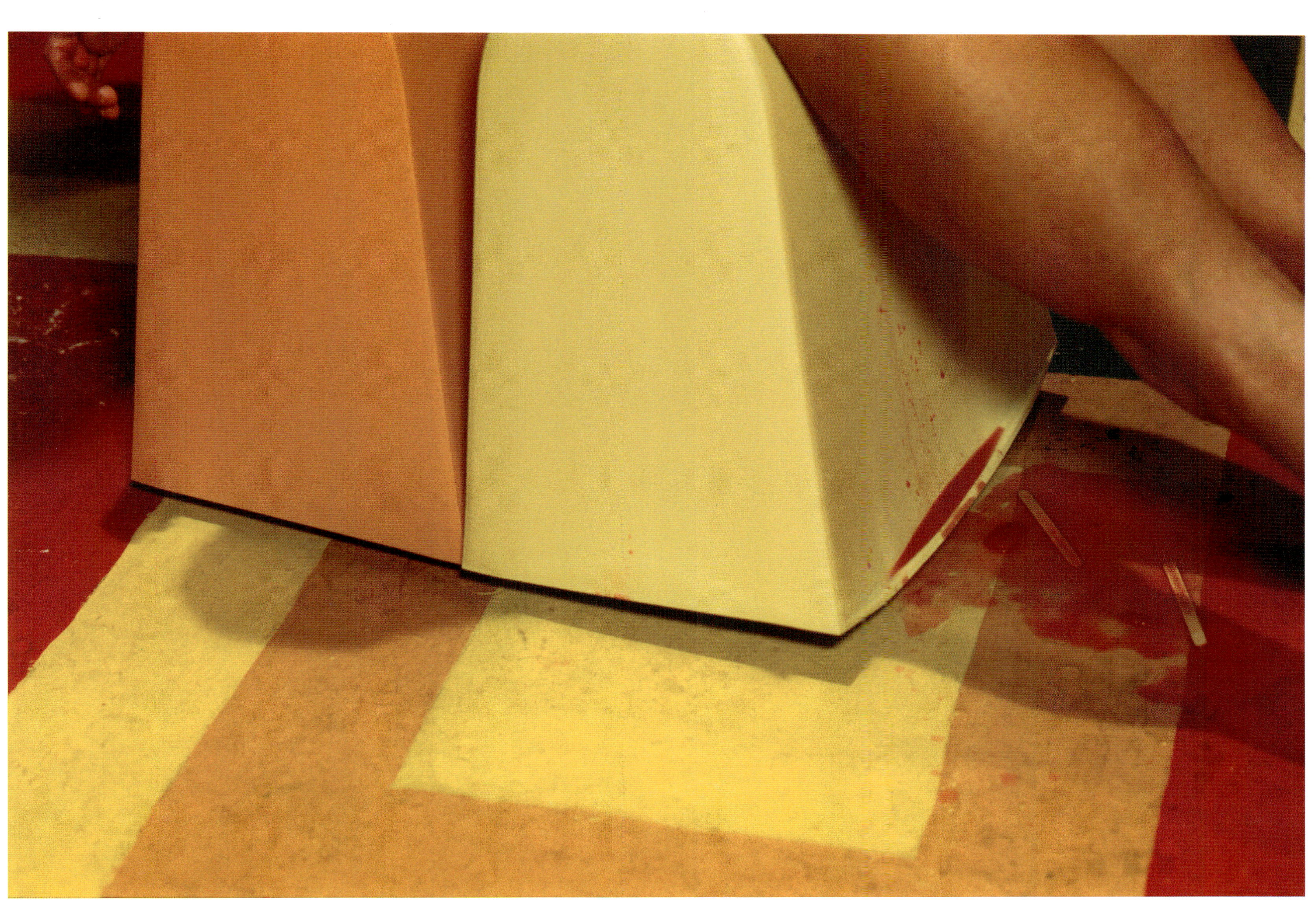

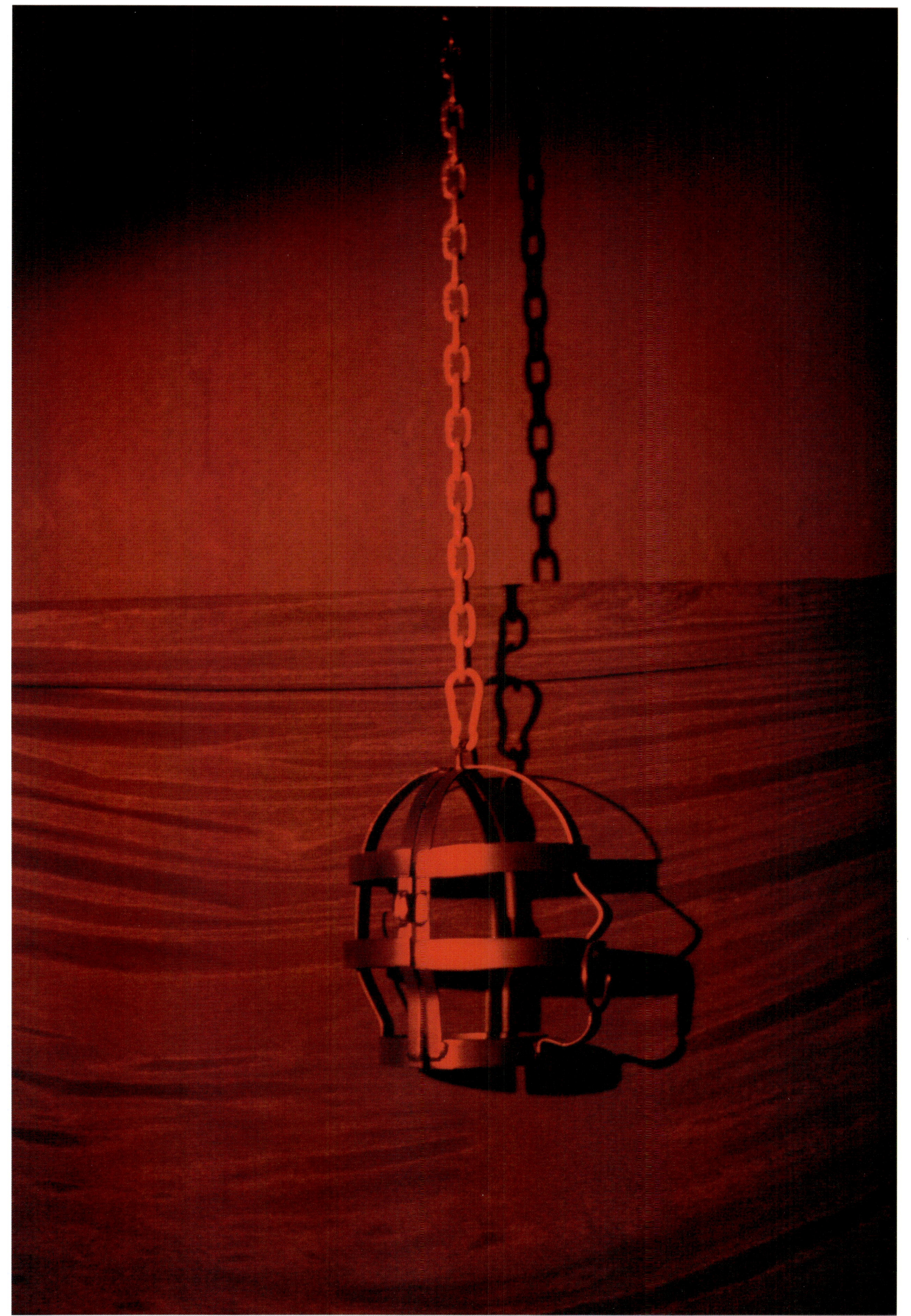

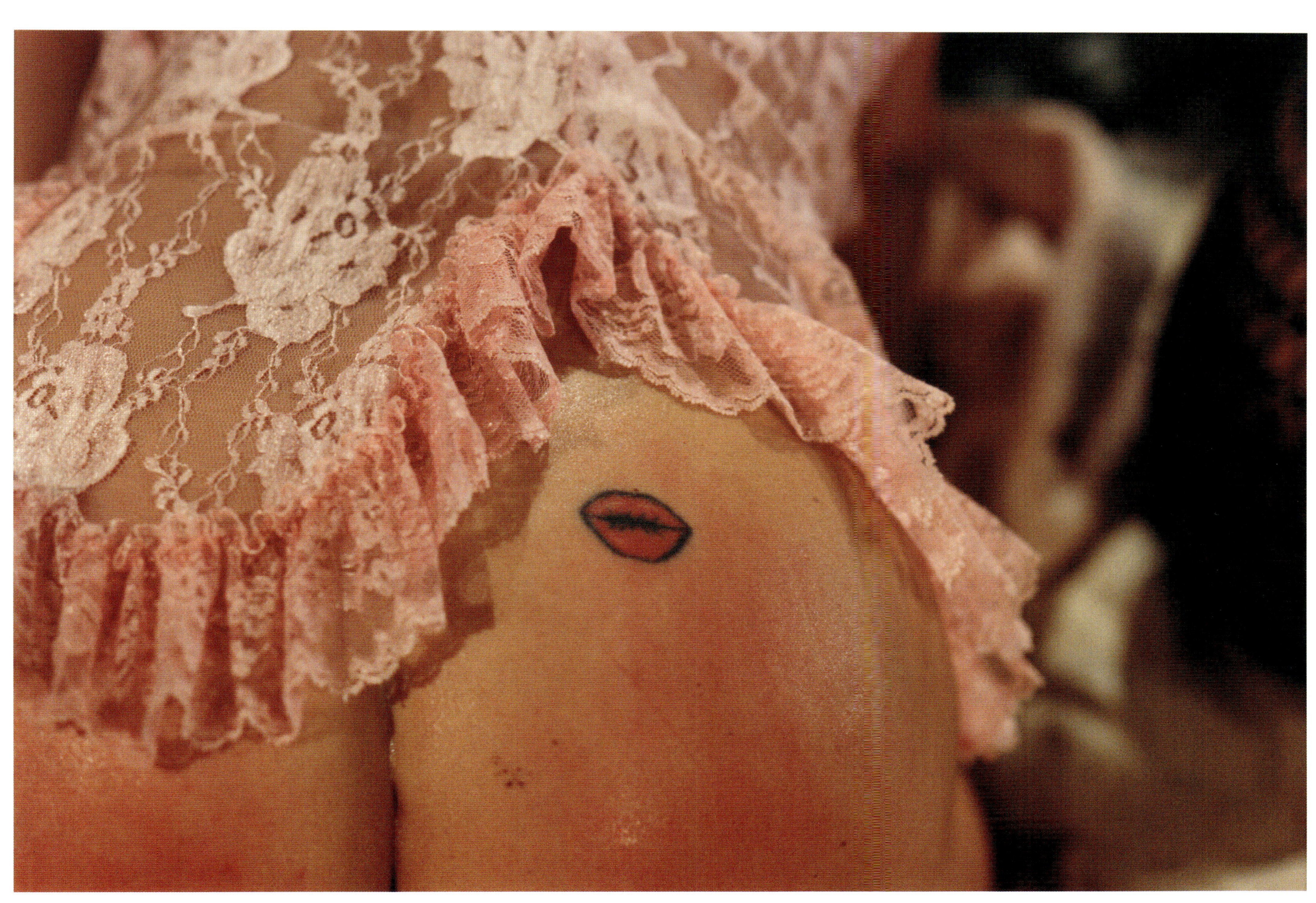

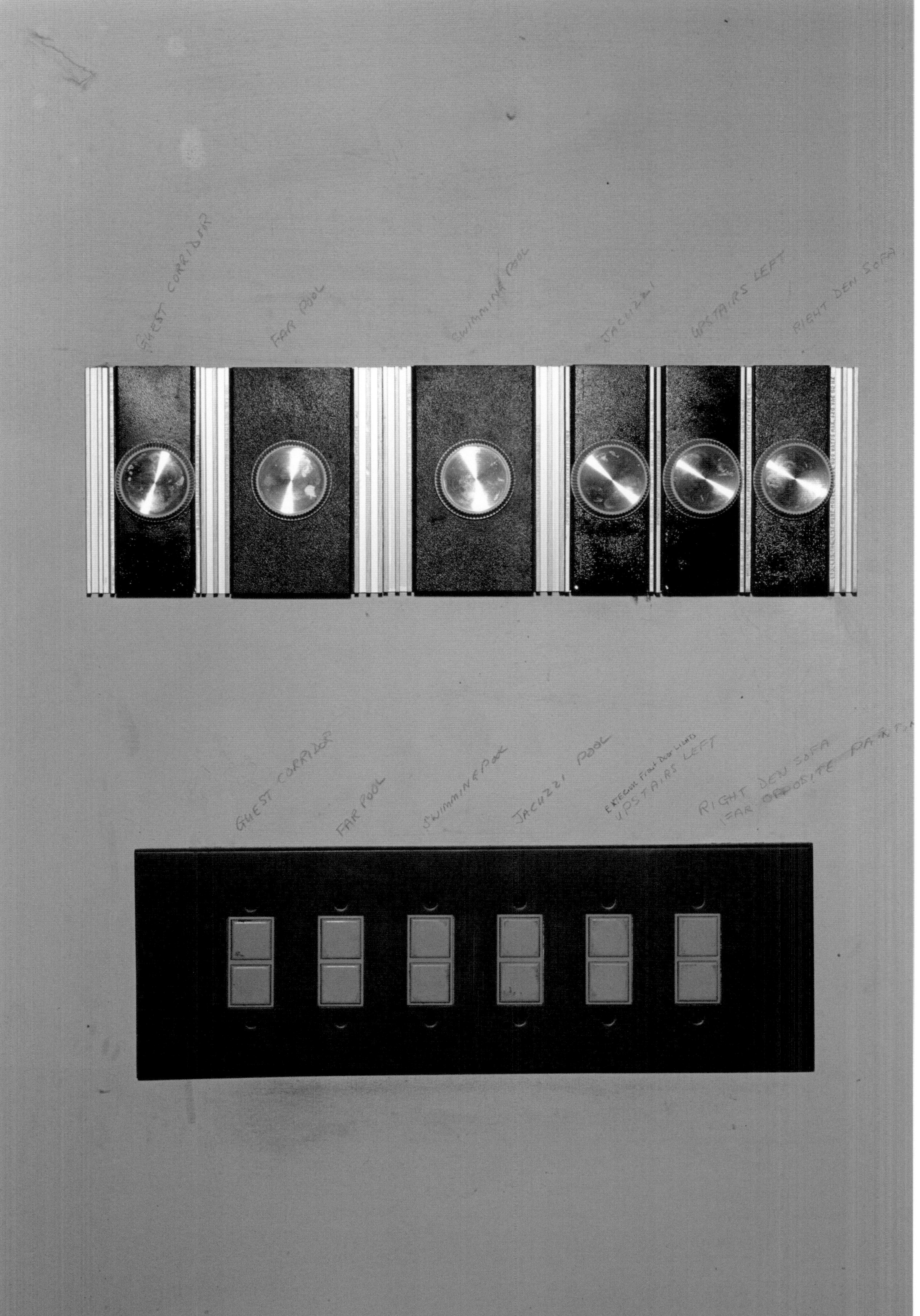

GUEST CORRIDOR
FAR POOL
SWIMMING POOL
JACUZZI
UPSTAIRS LEFT
RIGHT DEN SOFA
GUEST CORRIDOR
FAR POOL
SWIMMING POOL
JACUZZI POOL
EXTERIOR Front Door LIGHT
UPSTAIRS LEFT
RIGHT DEN SOFA
(FAR OPPOSITE PARTIAL

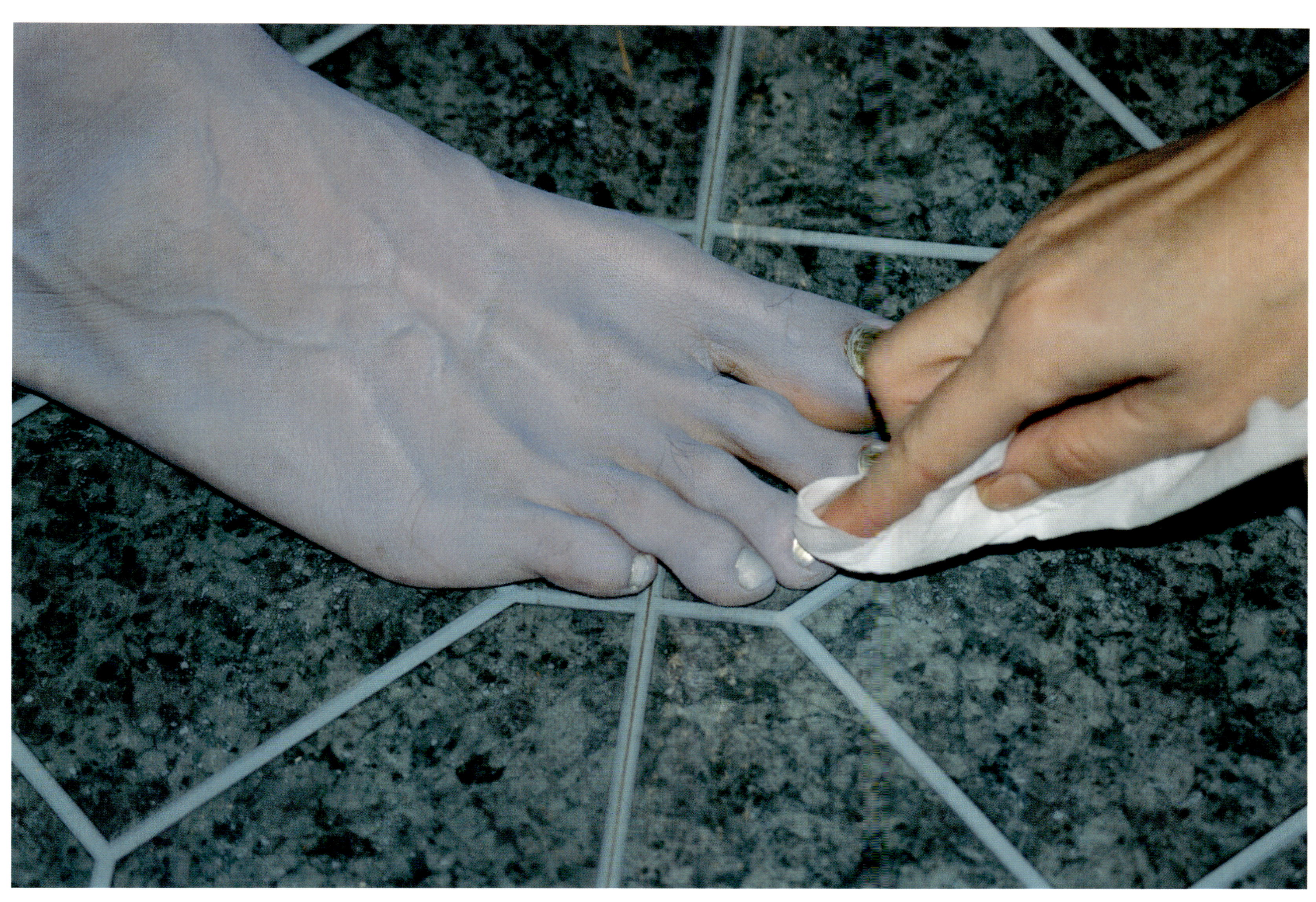

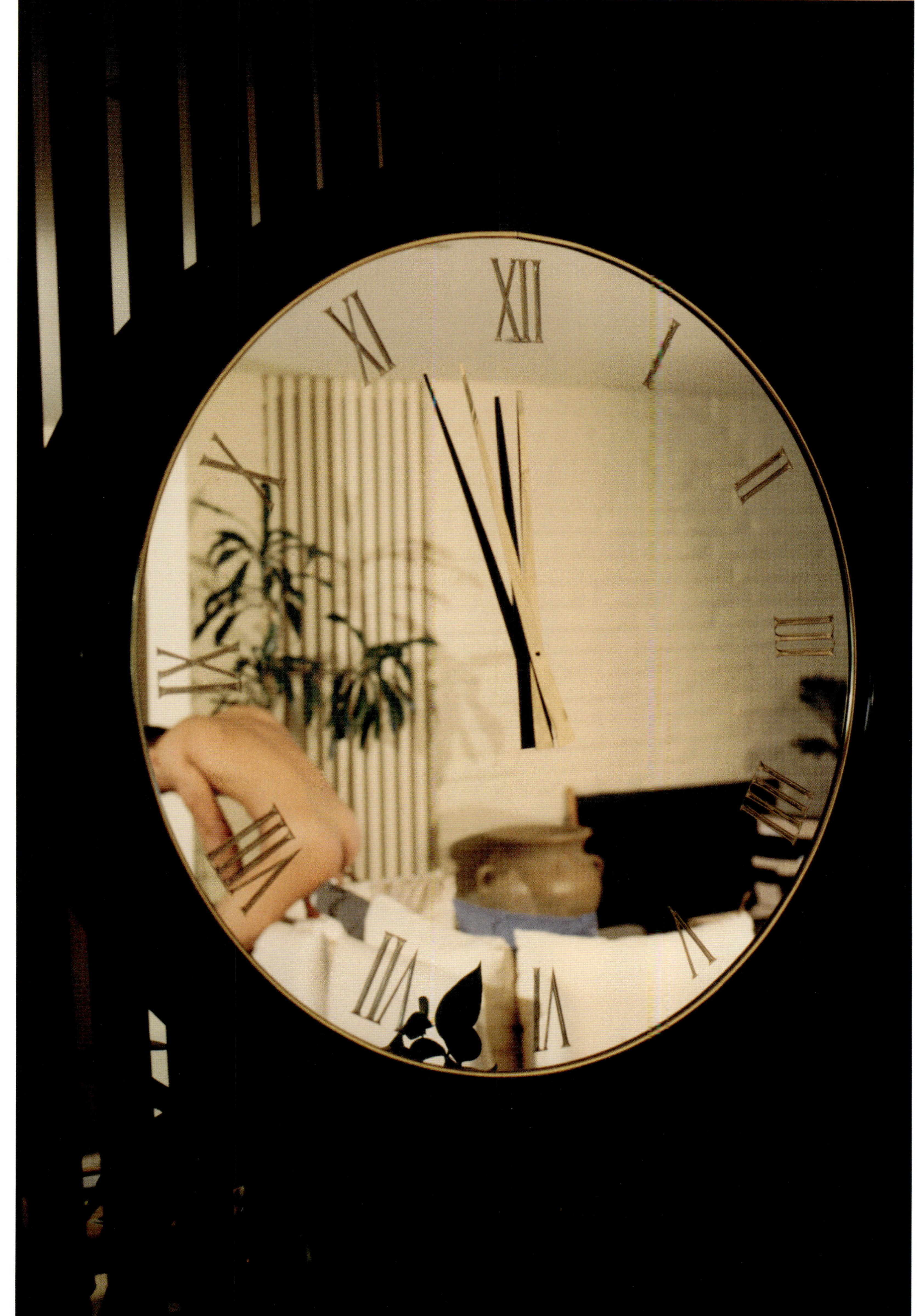

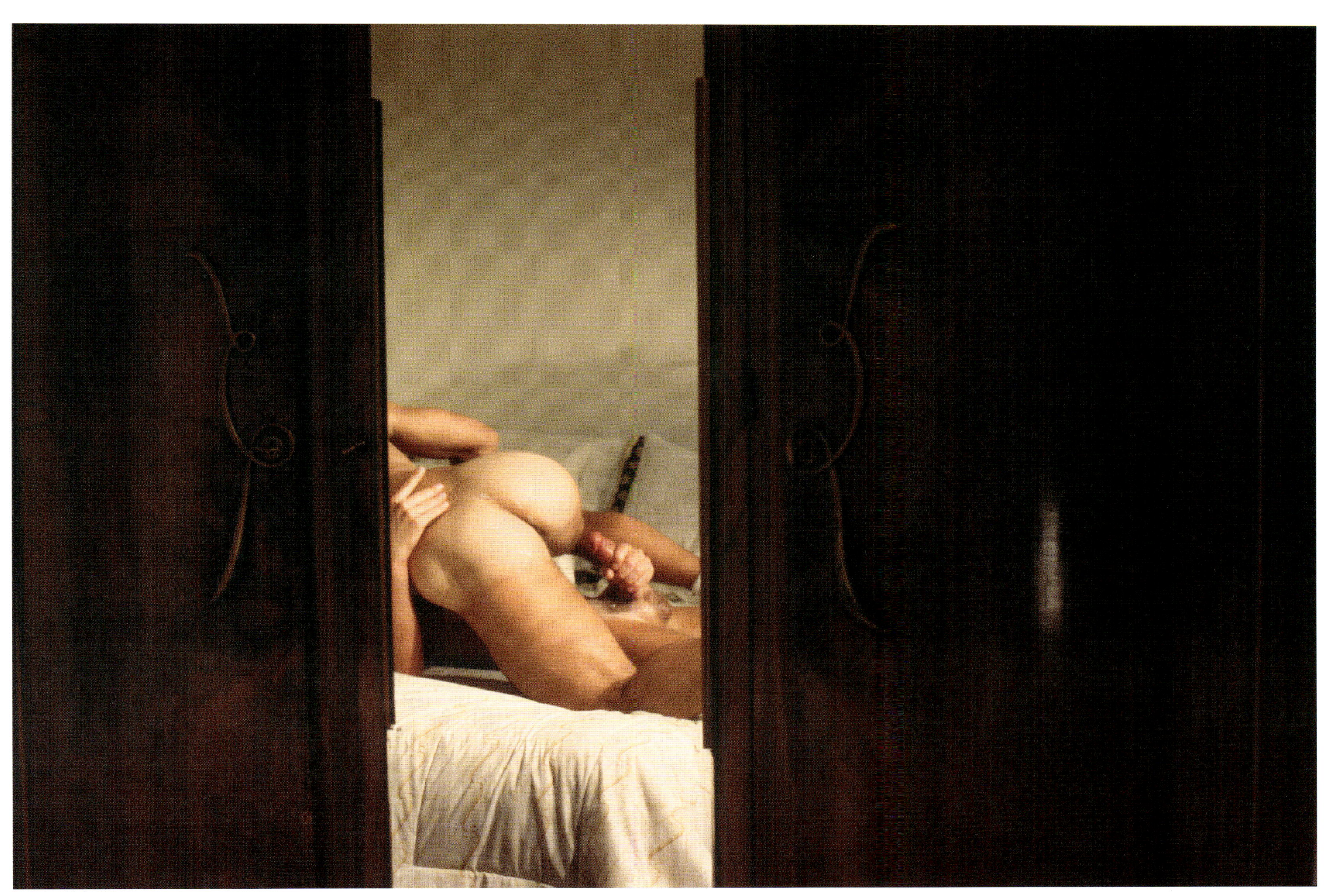

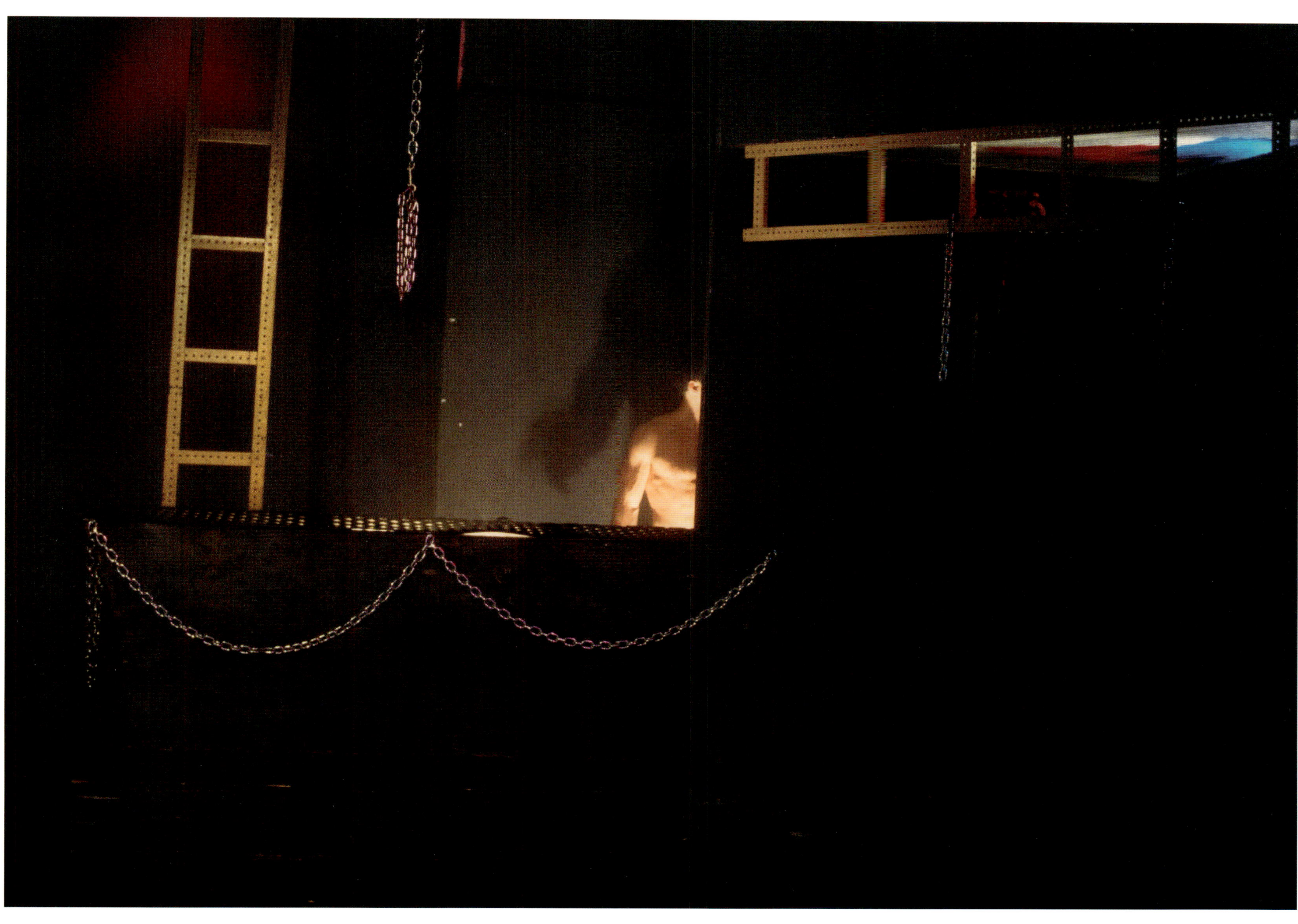

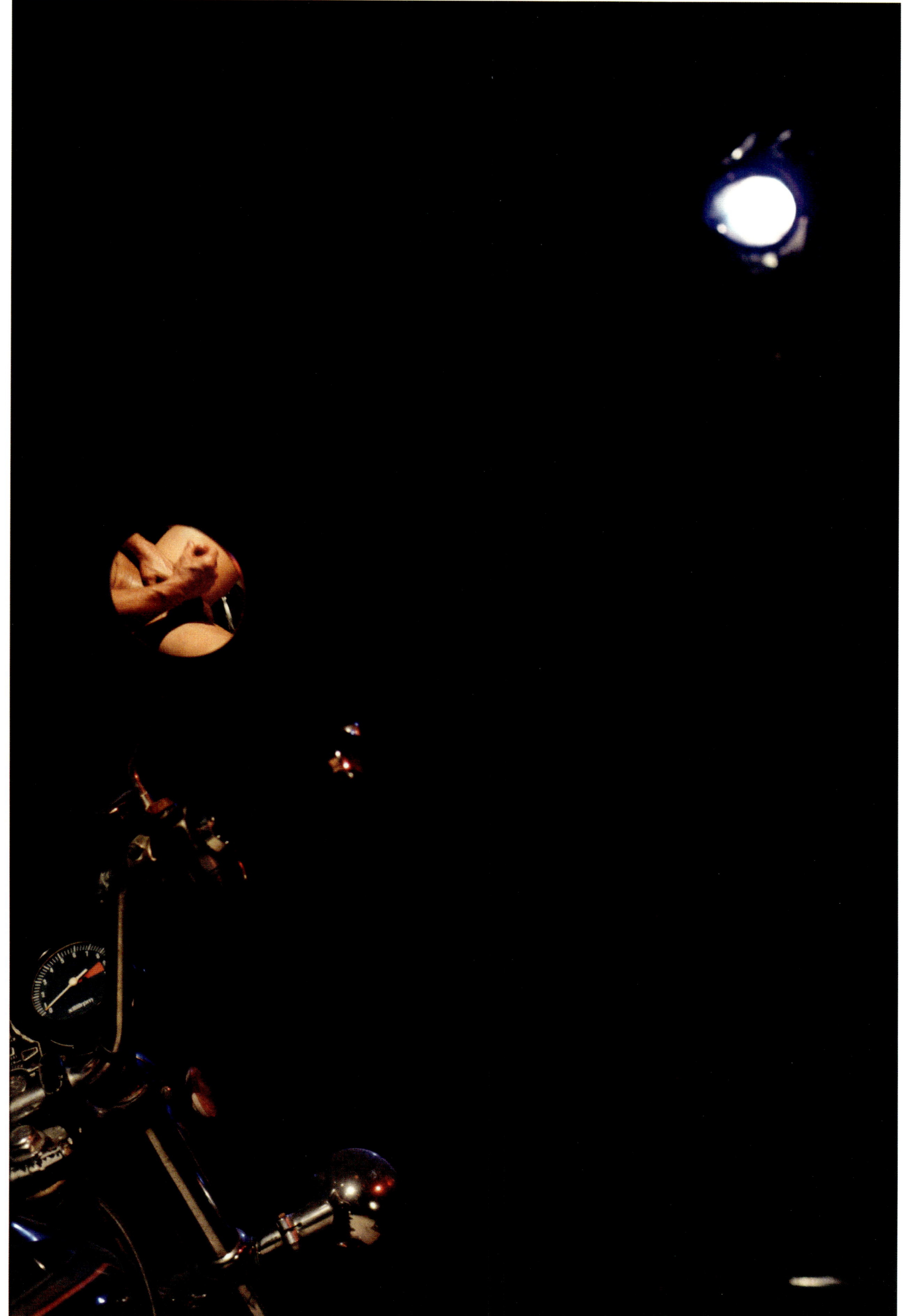

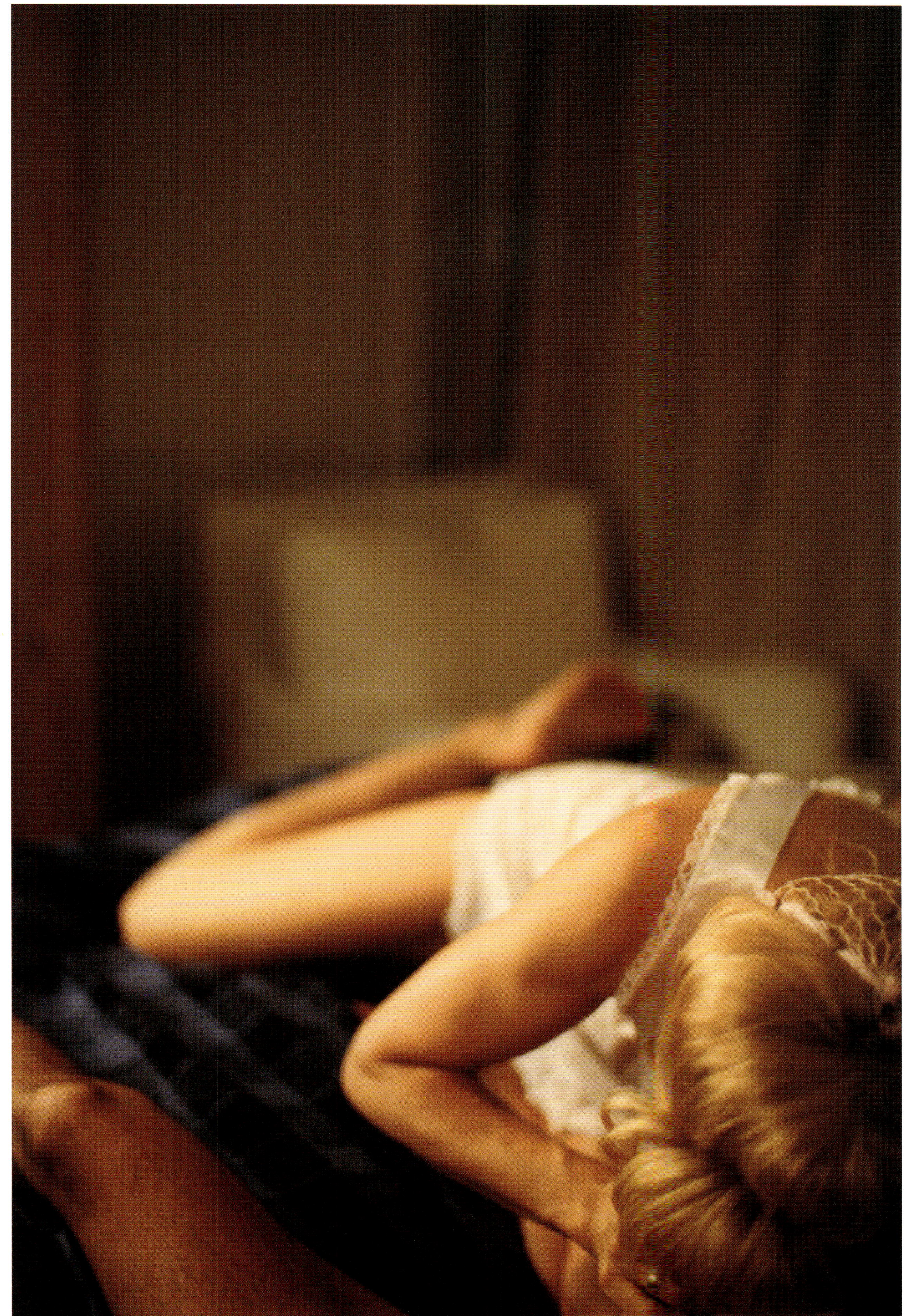

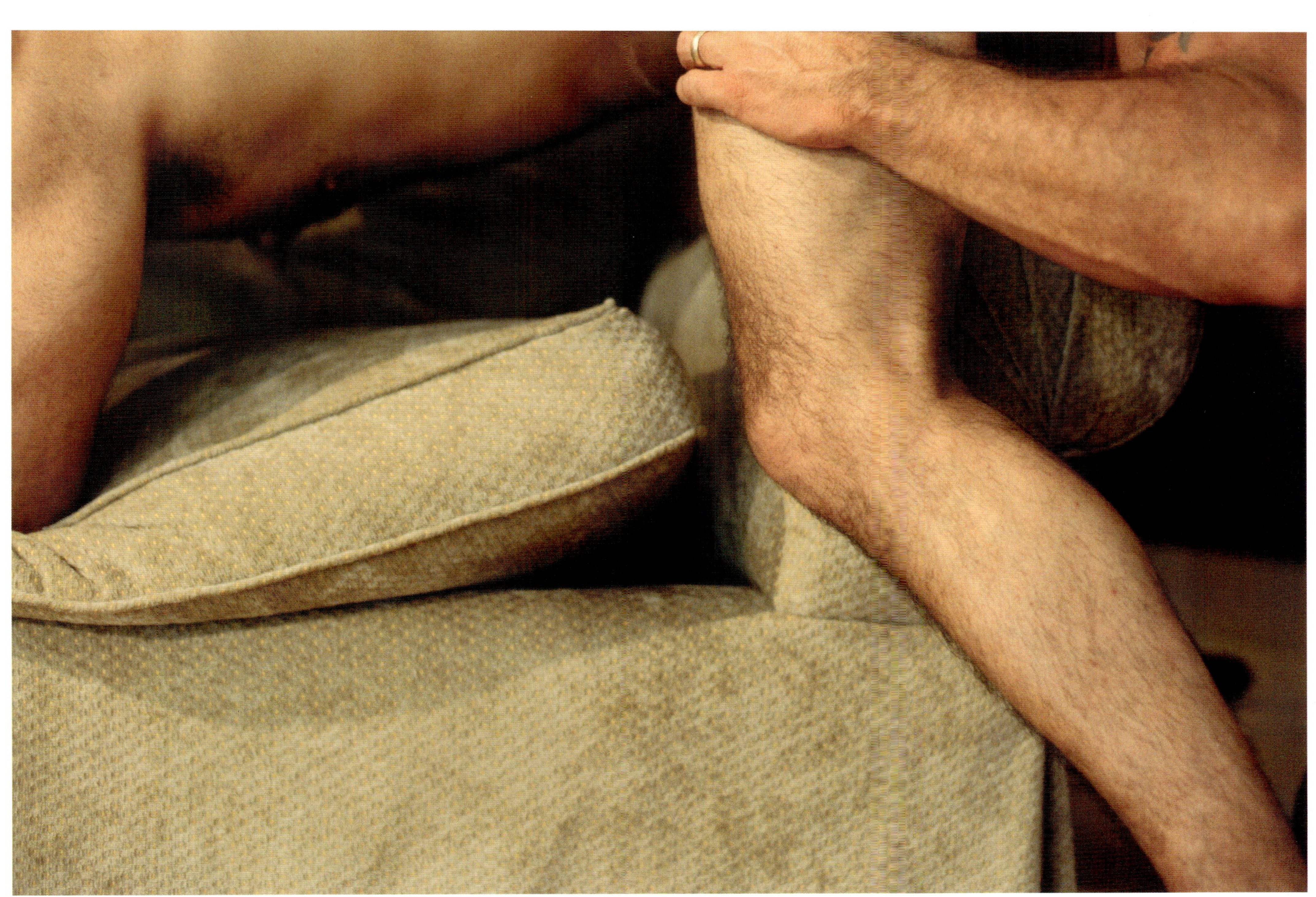

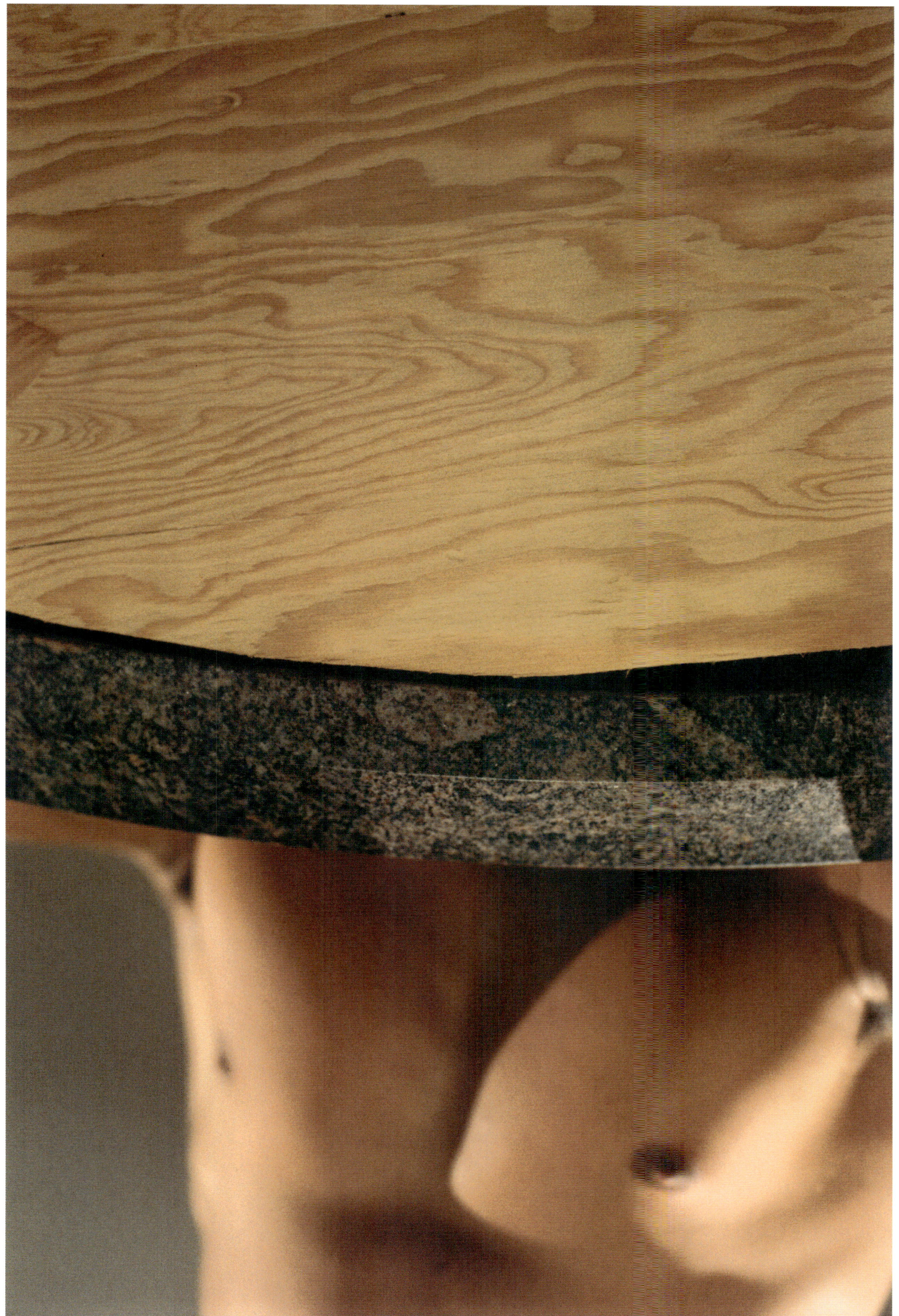

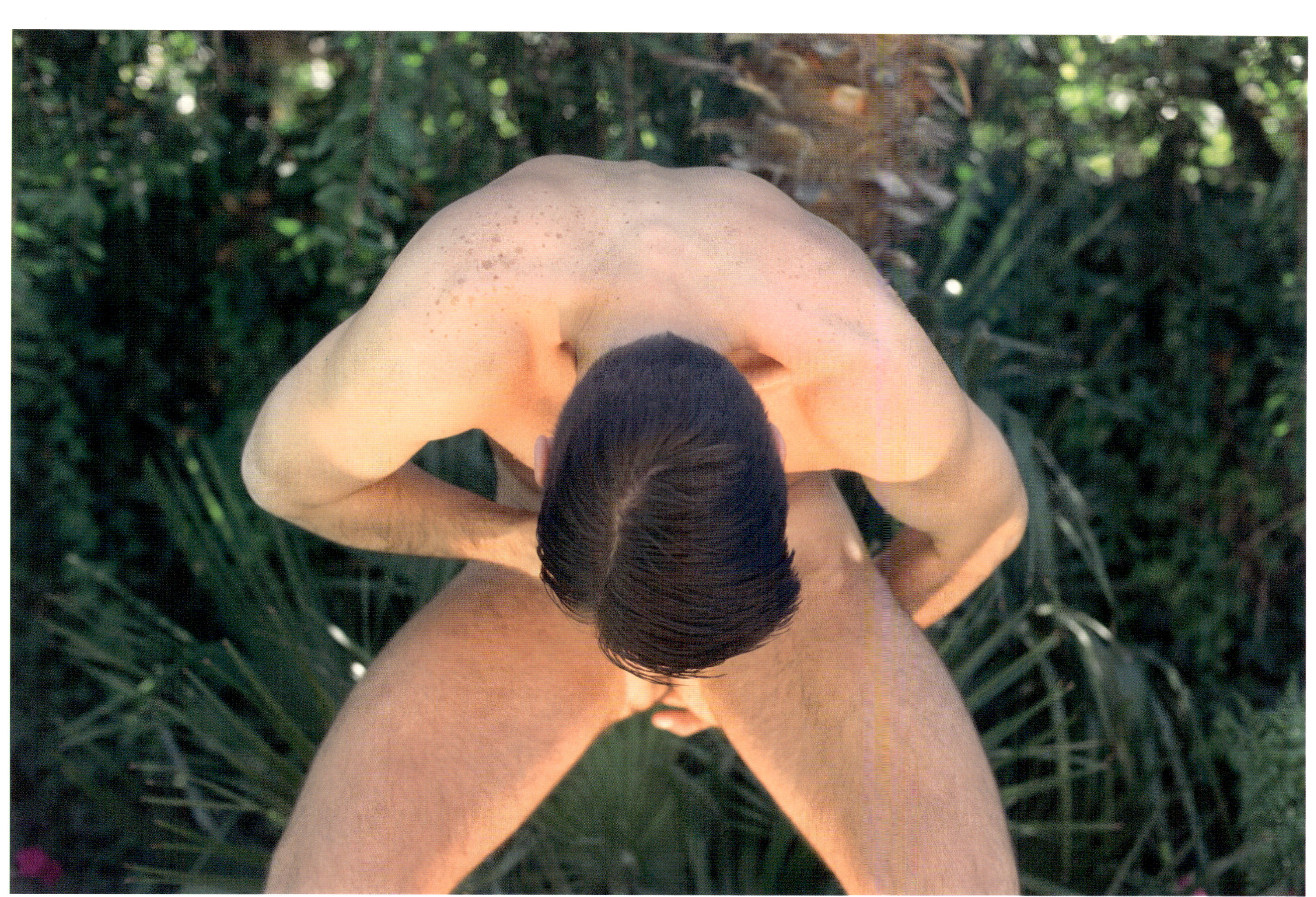

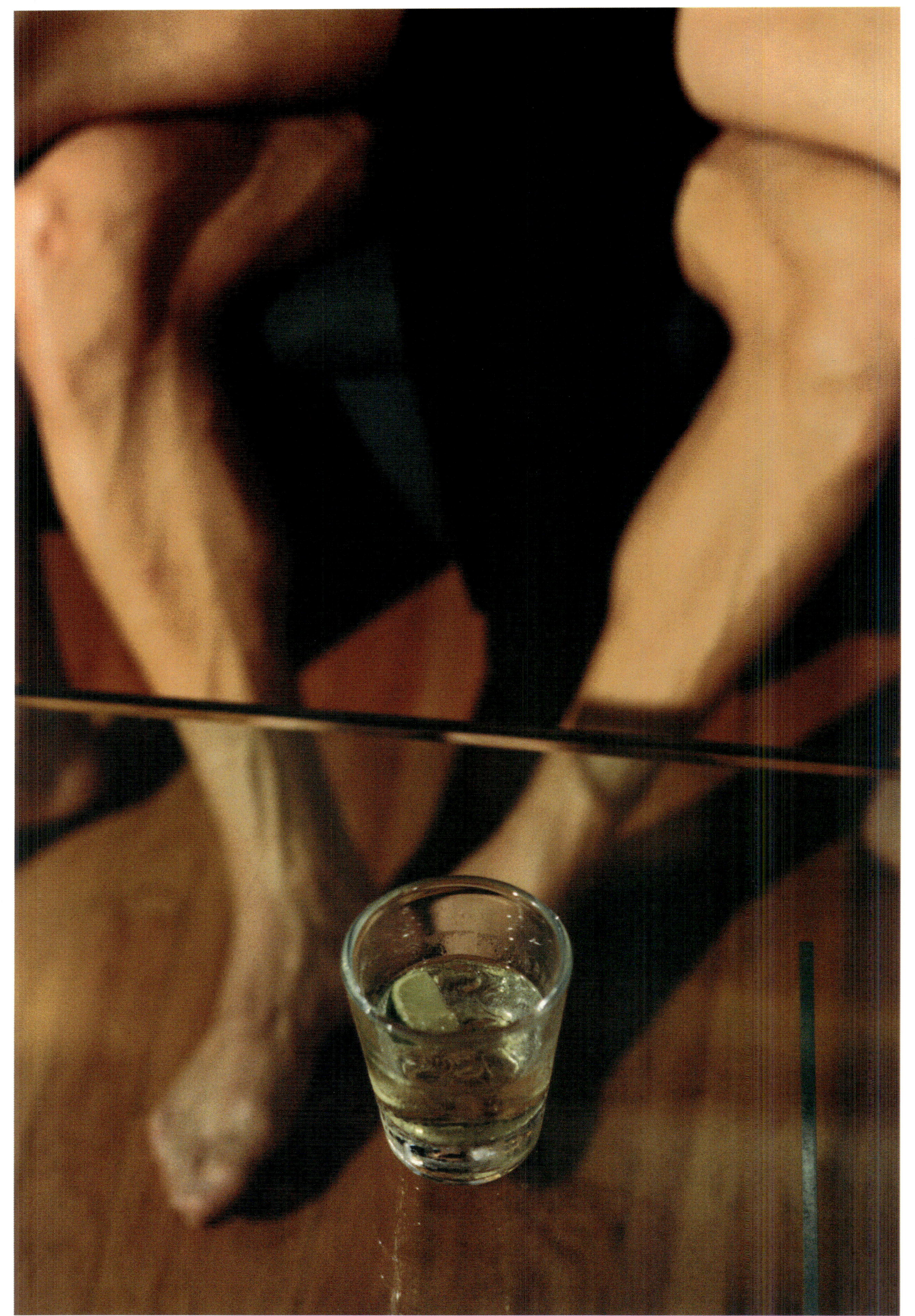

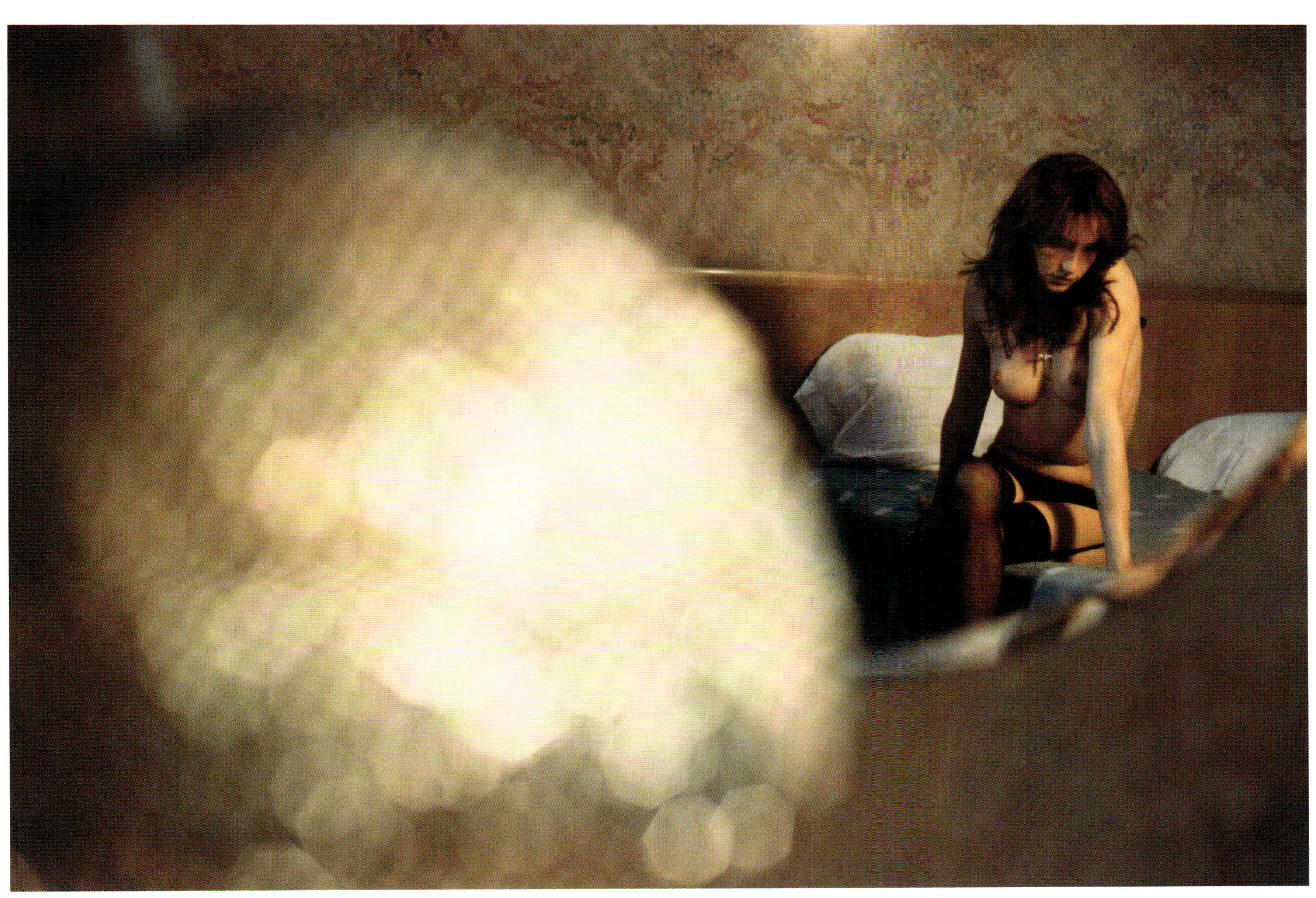

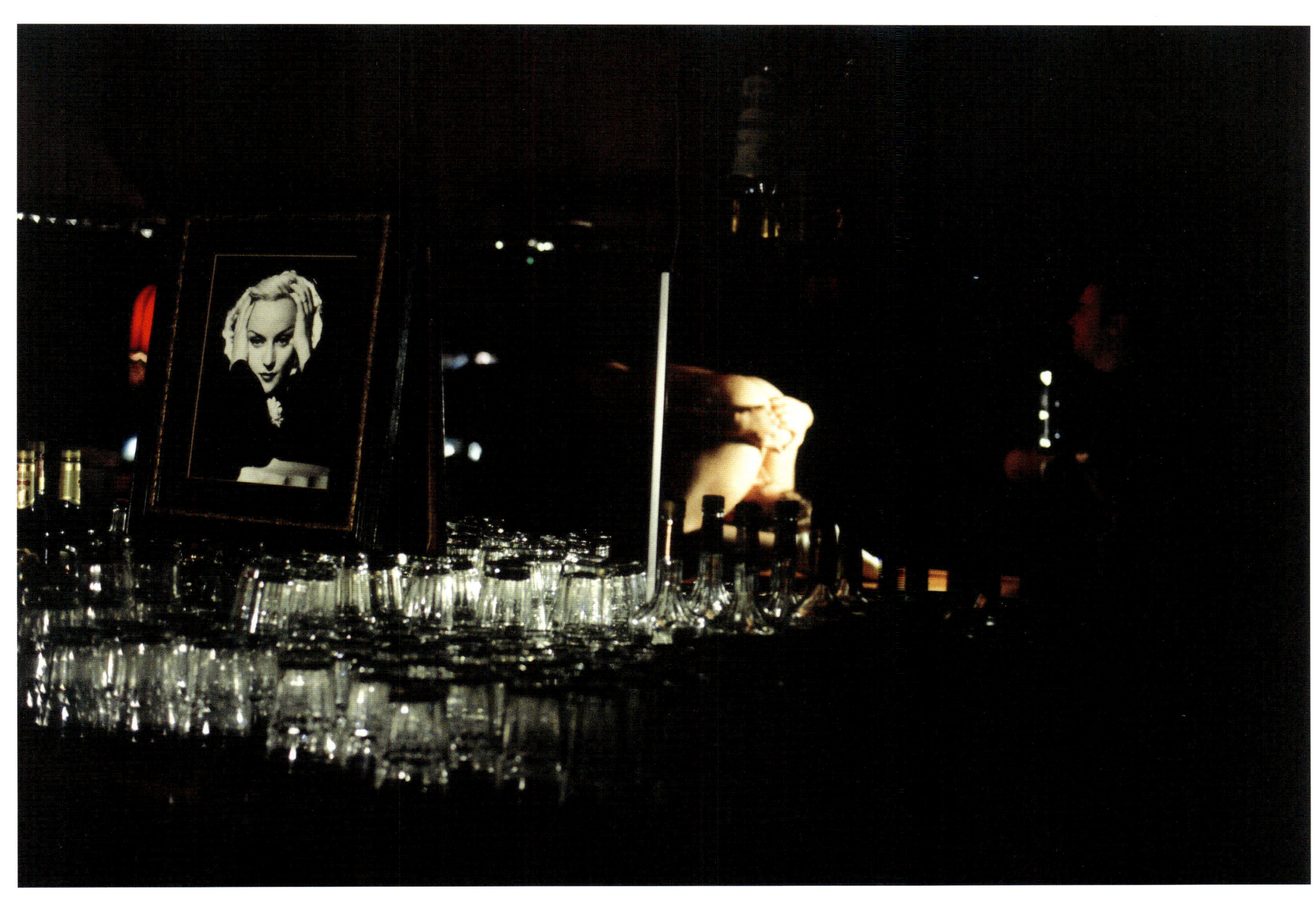

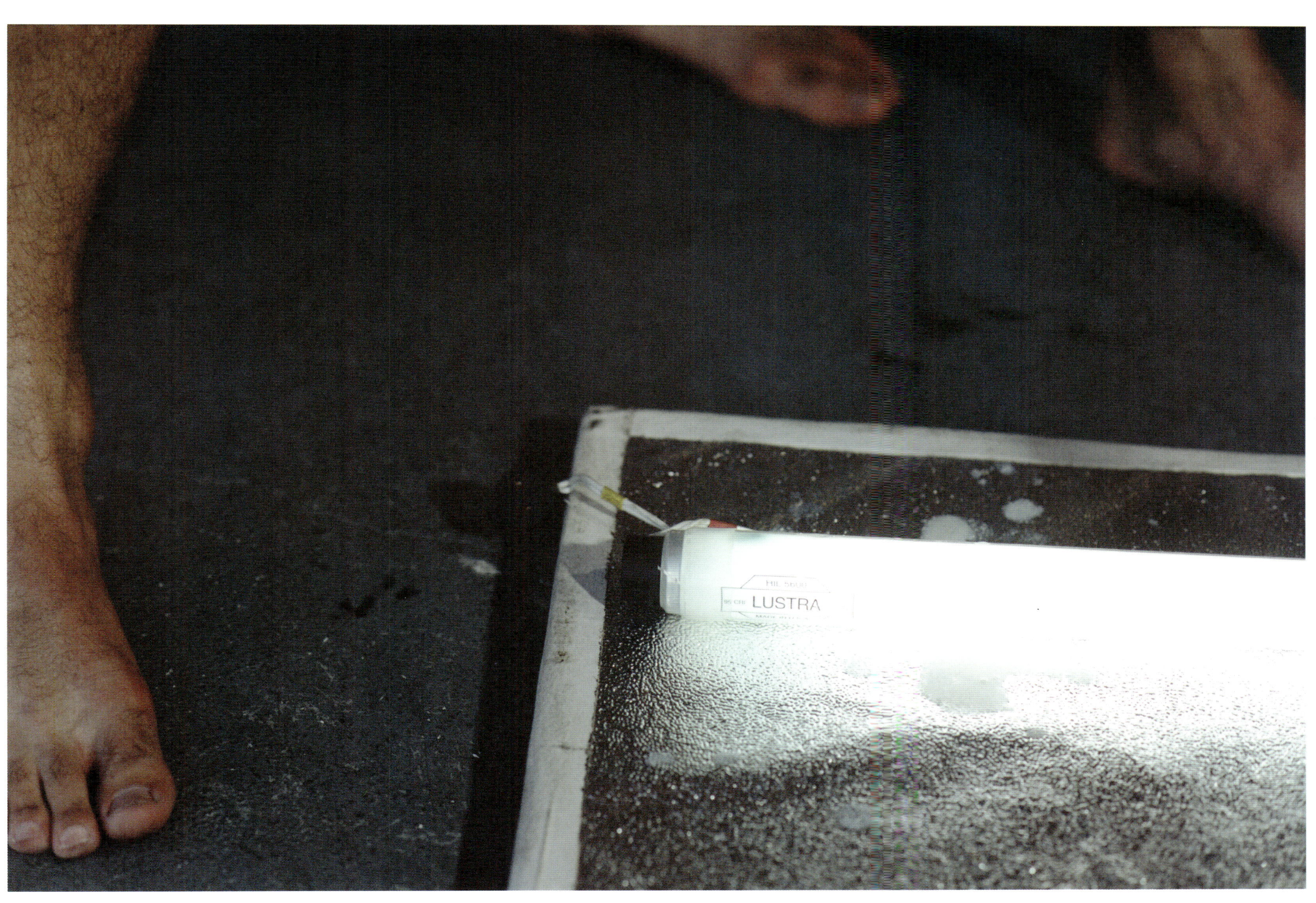

HIL 5600
95 CRI LUSTRA
MADE IN U.S.A.

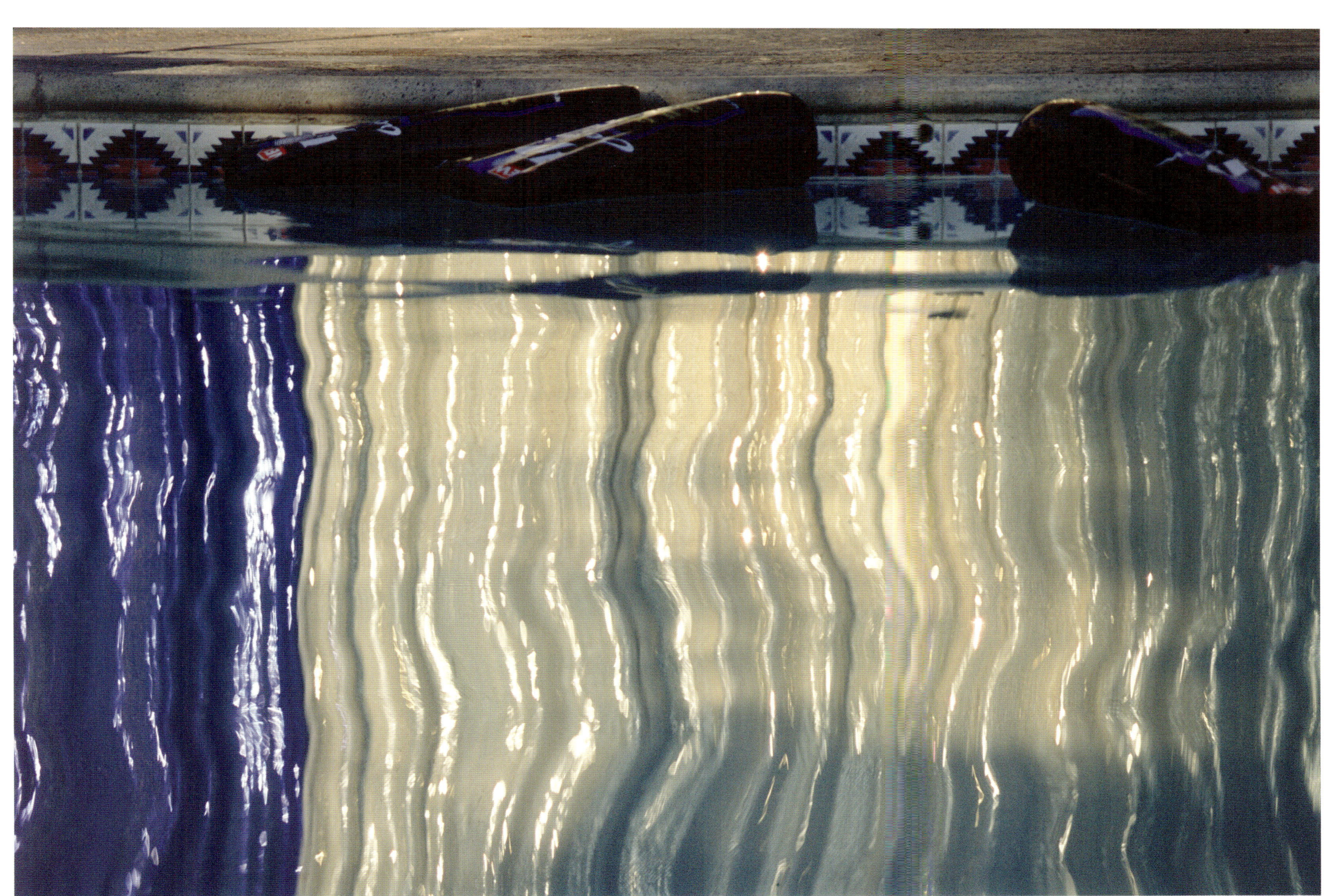

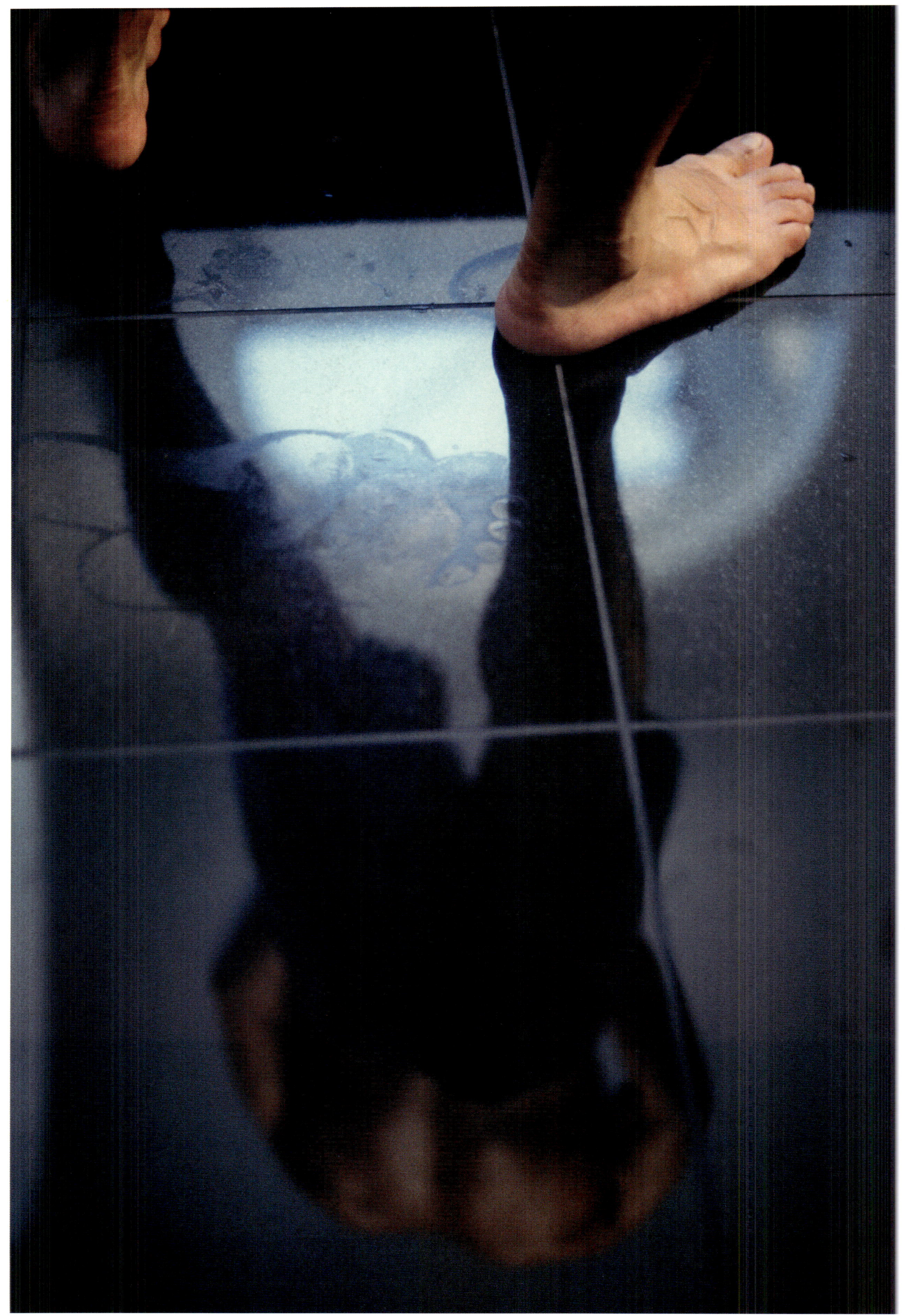

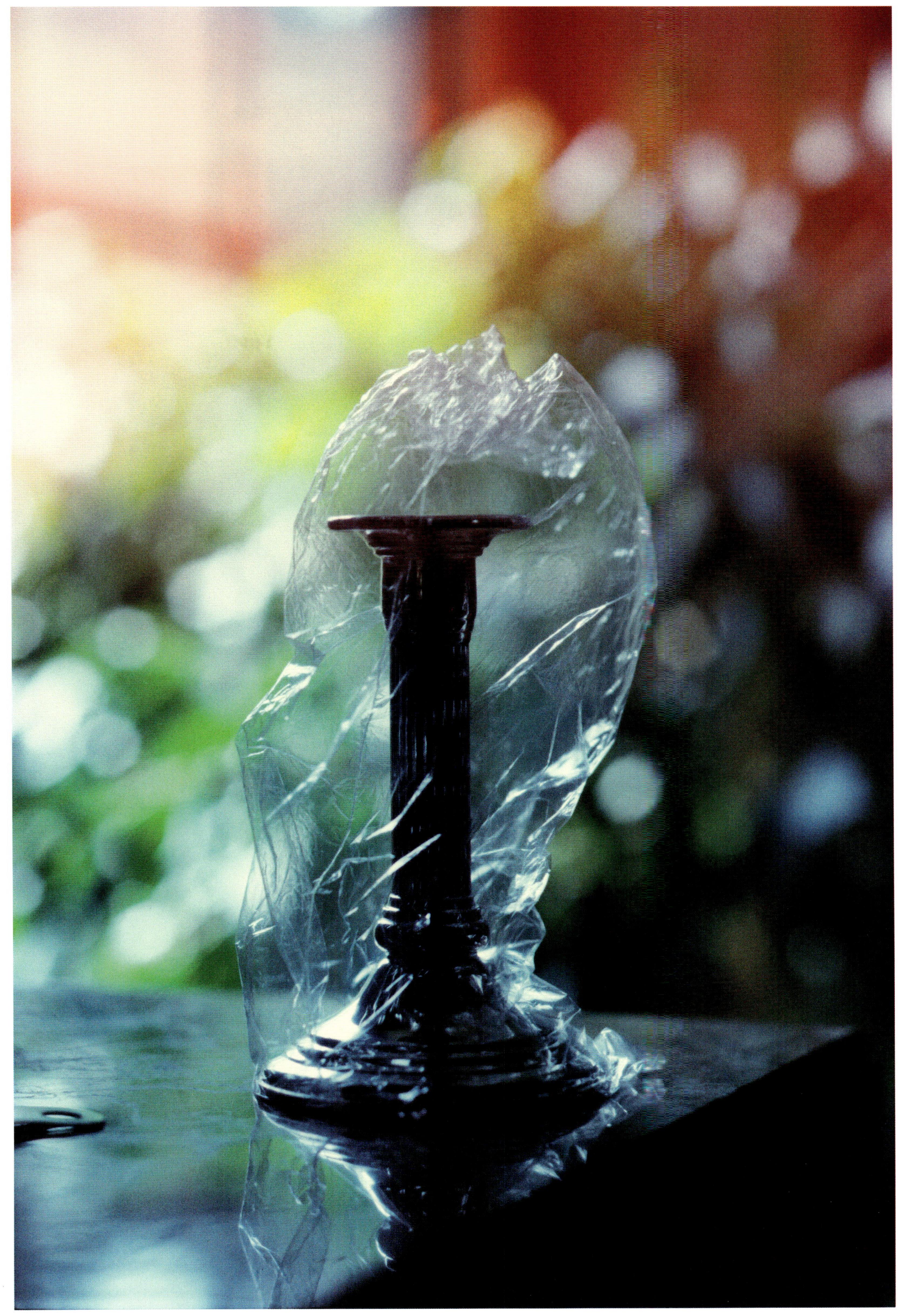

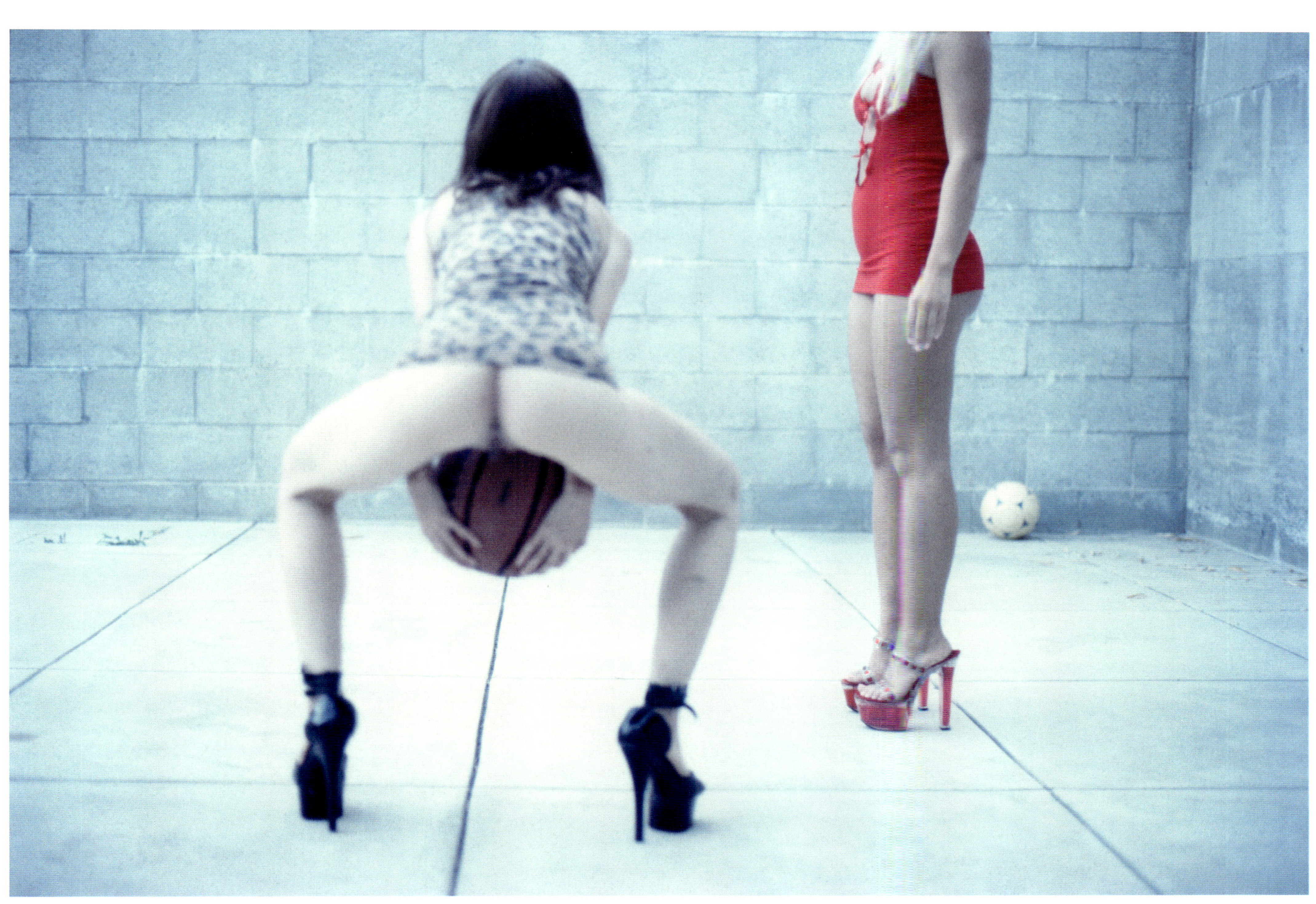

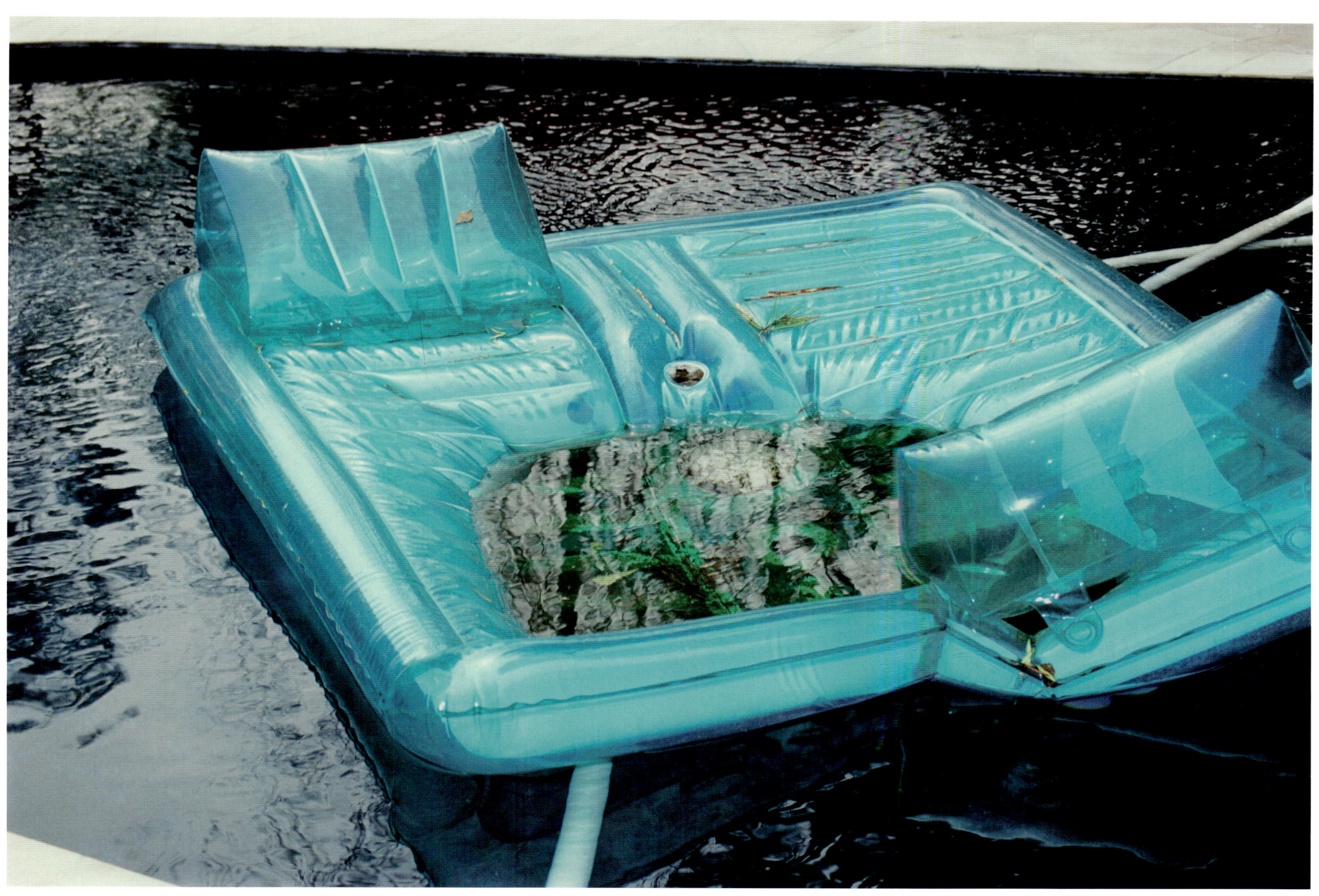

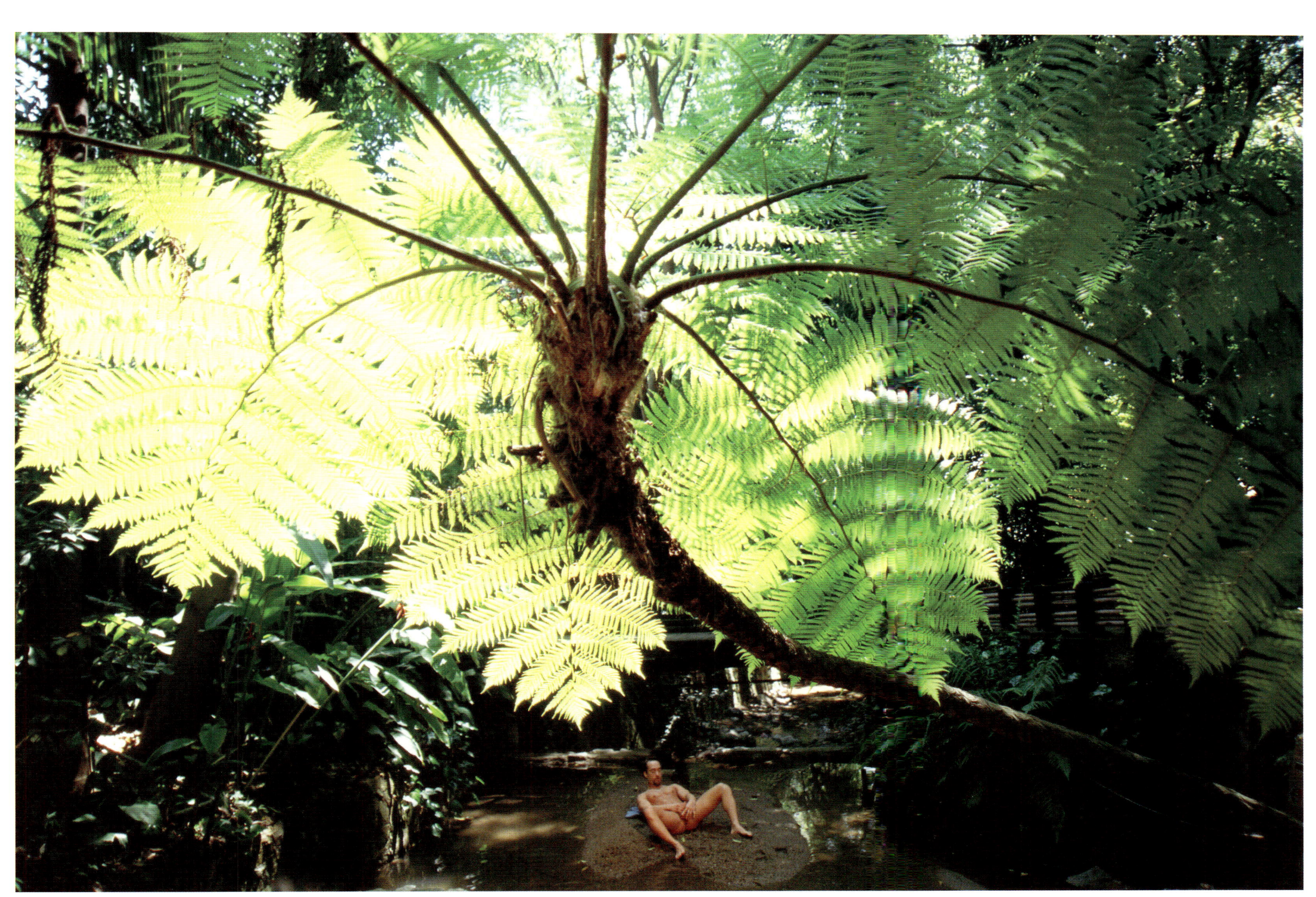

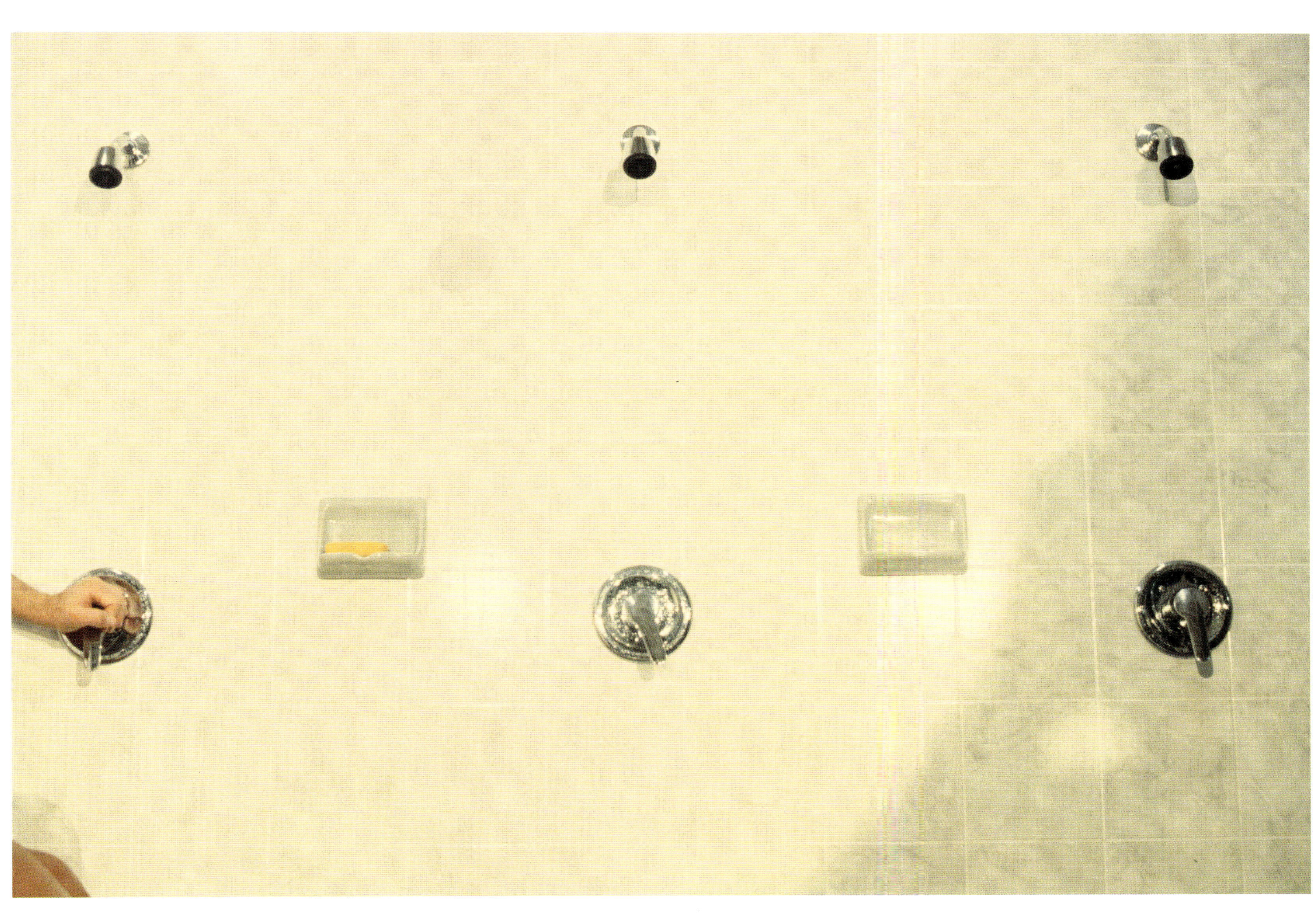

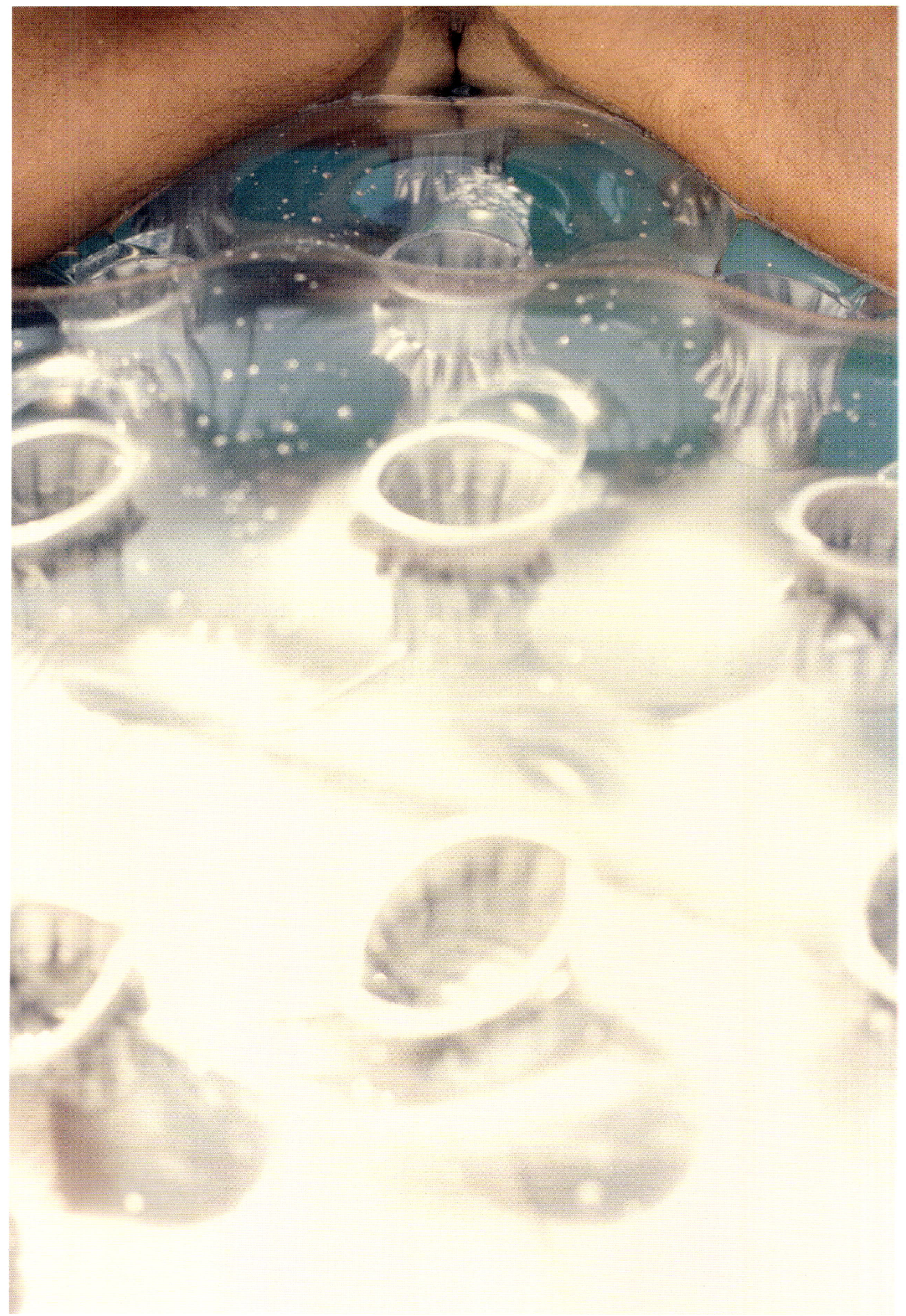

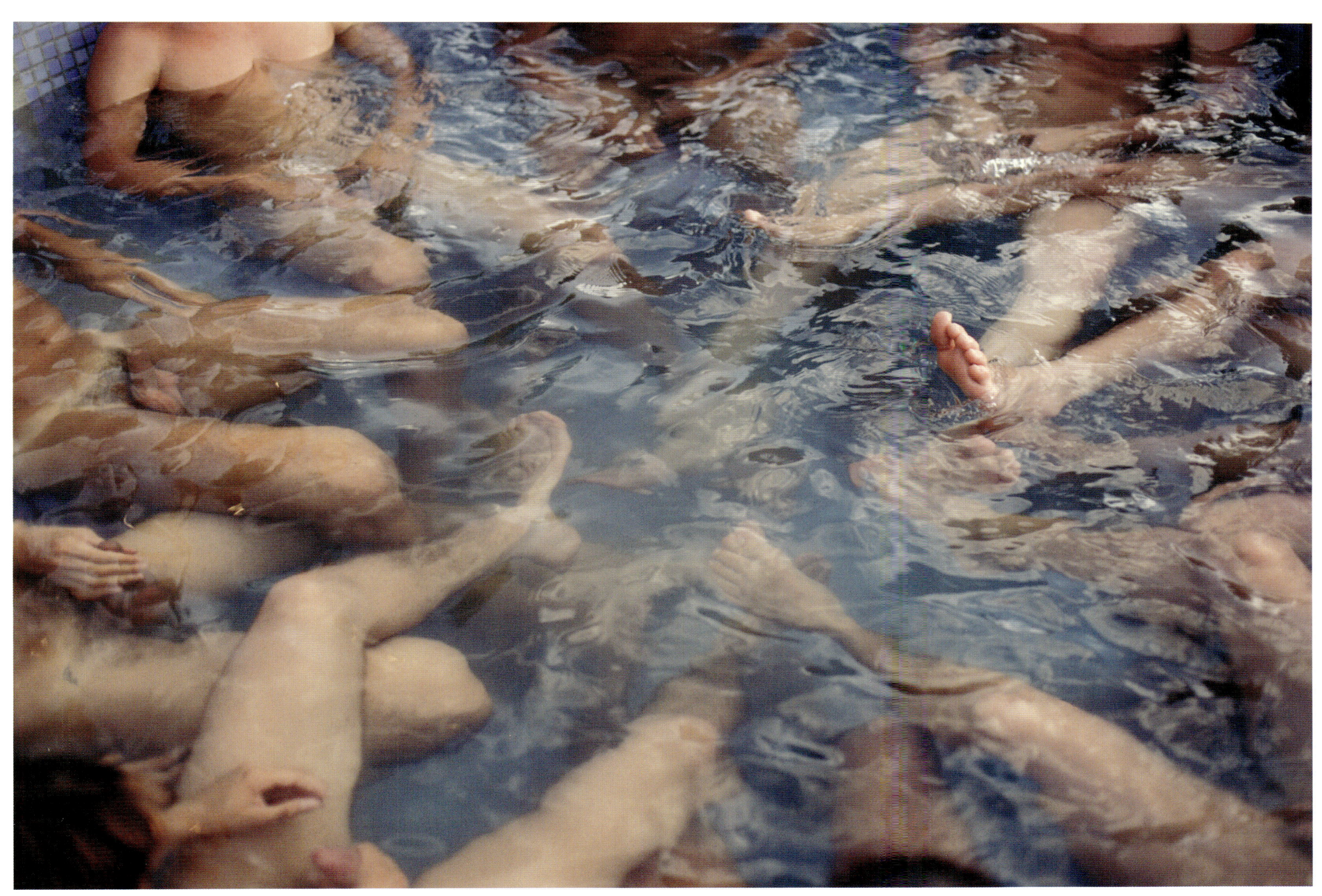

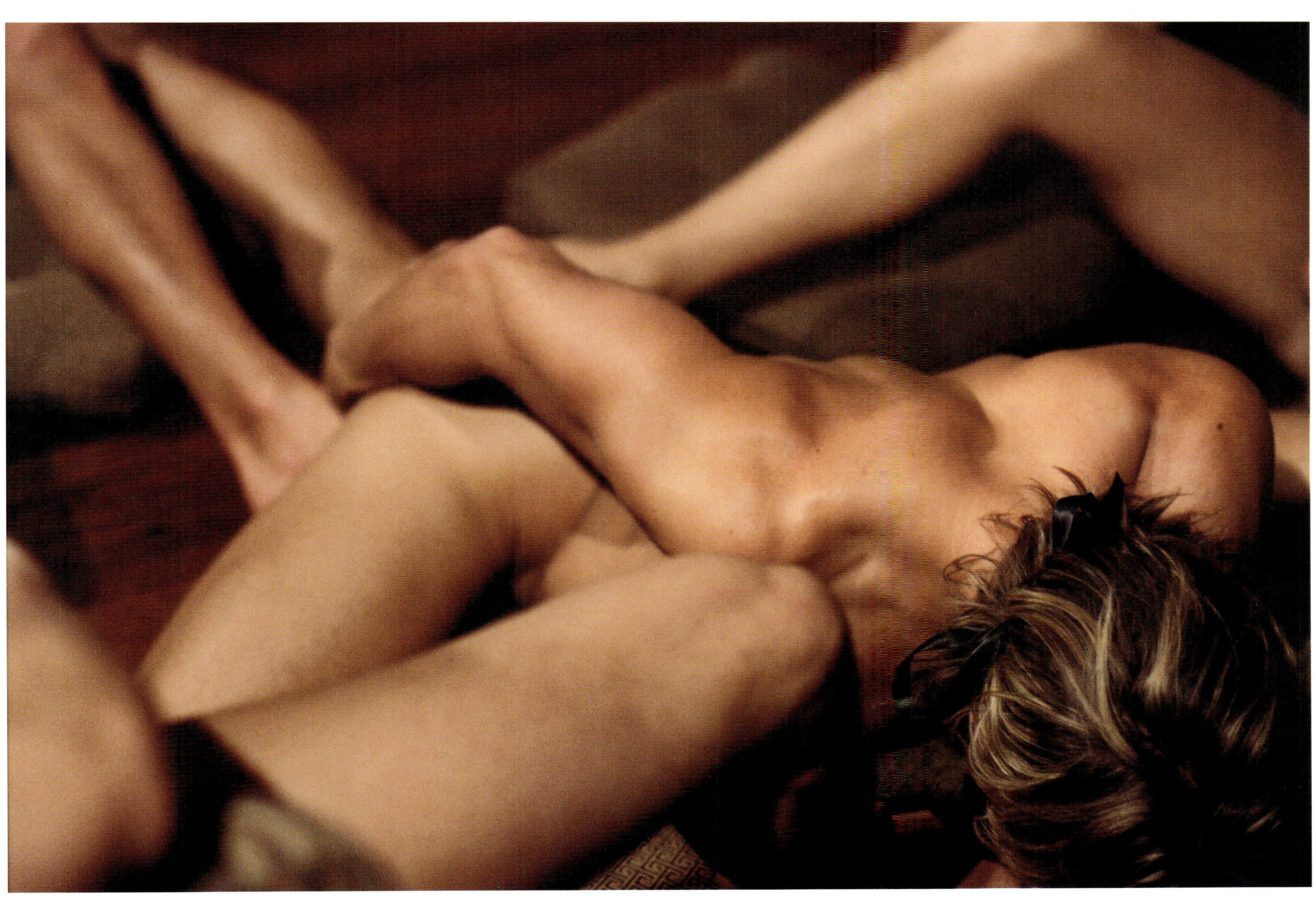

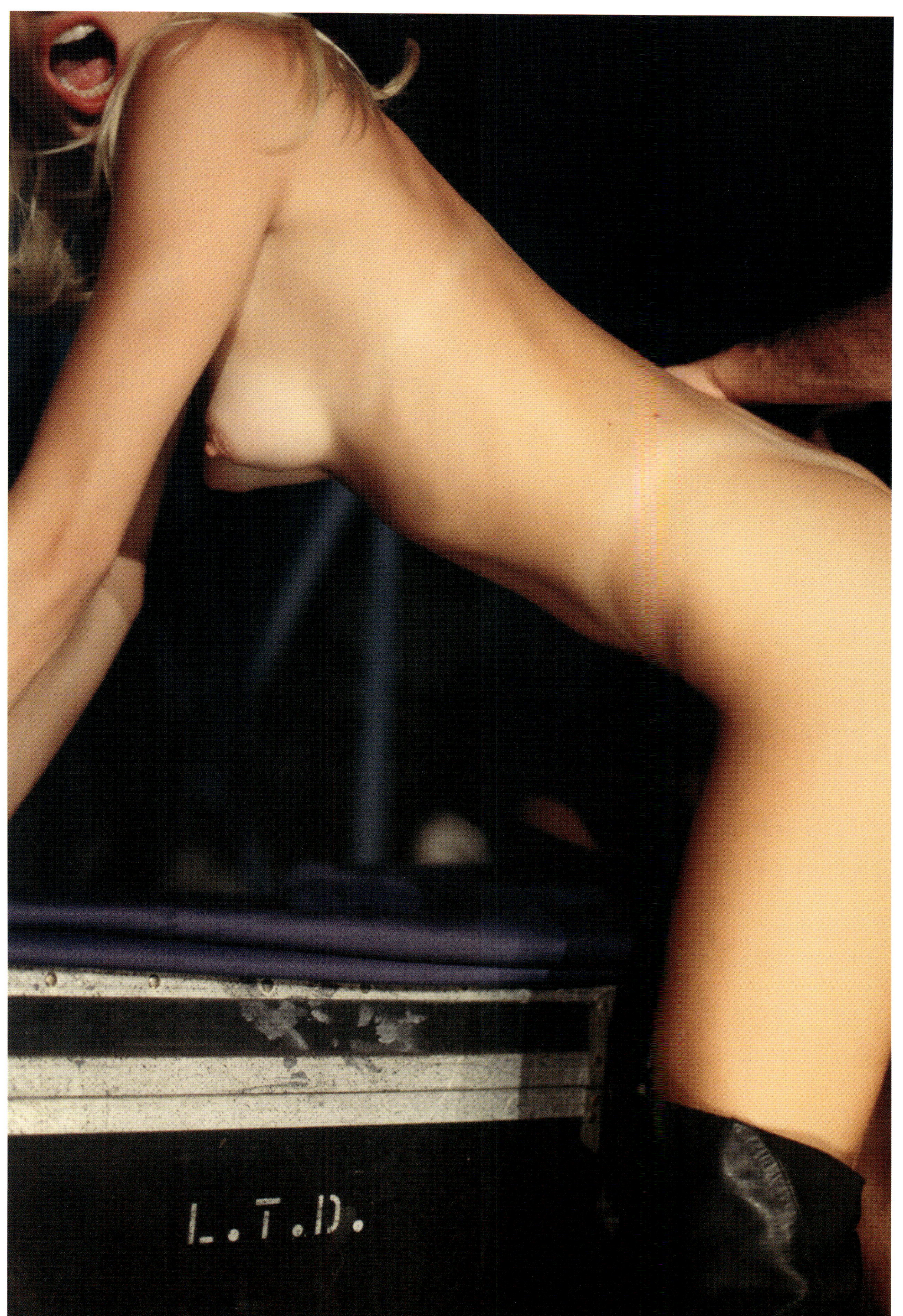

L.T.D.

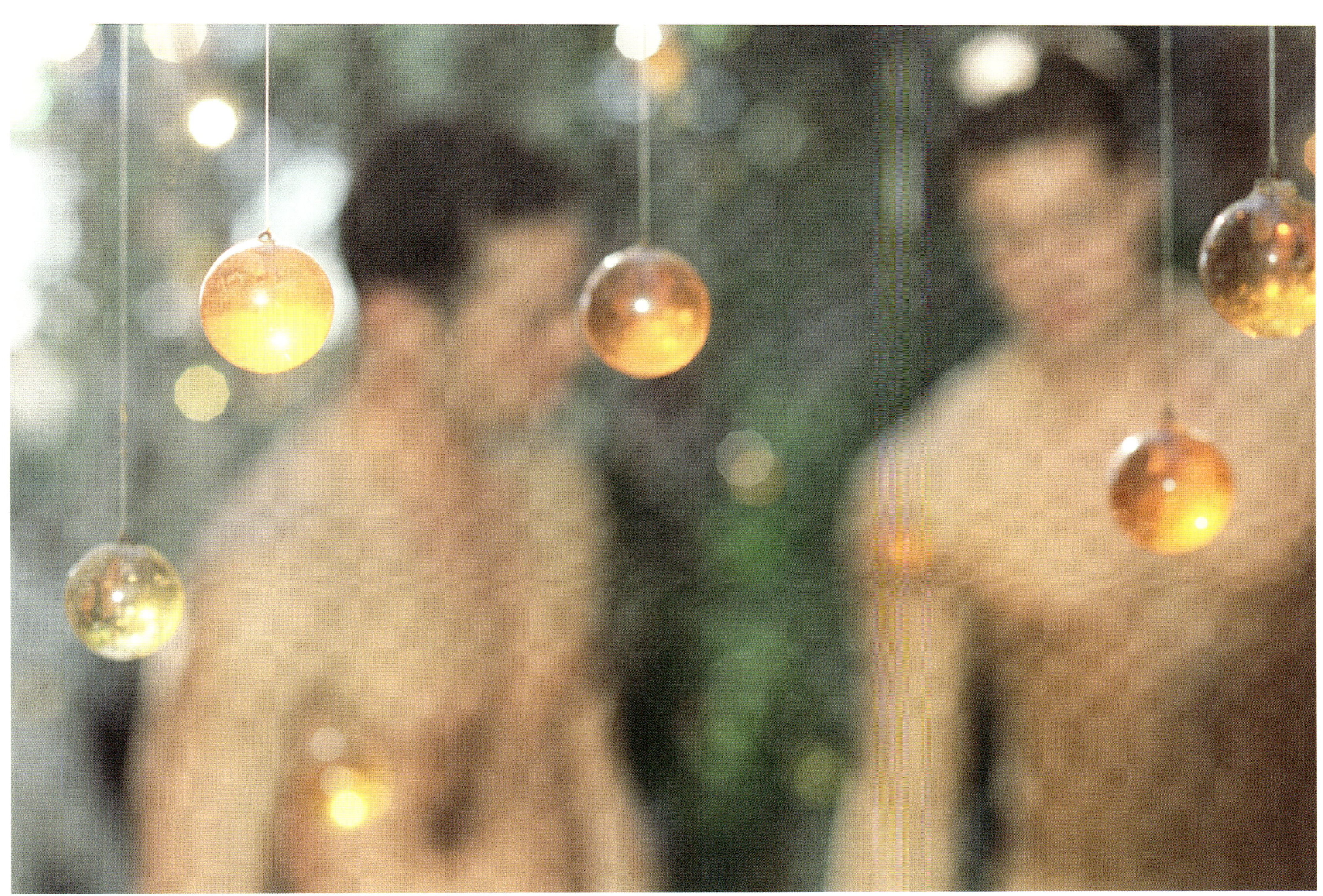

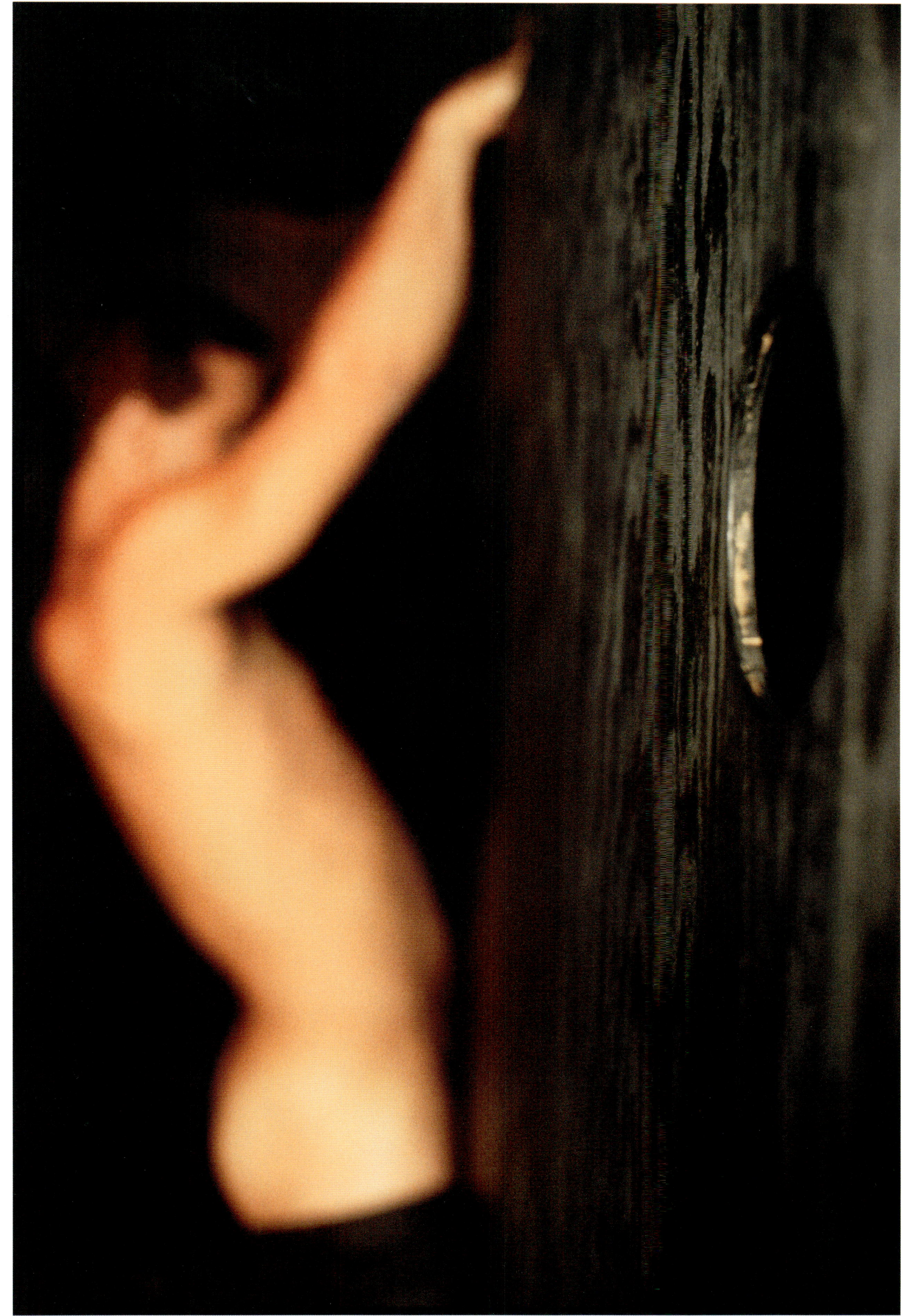

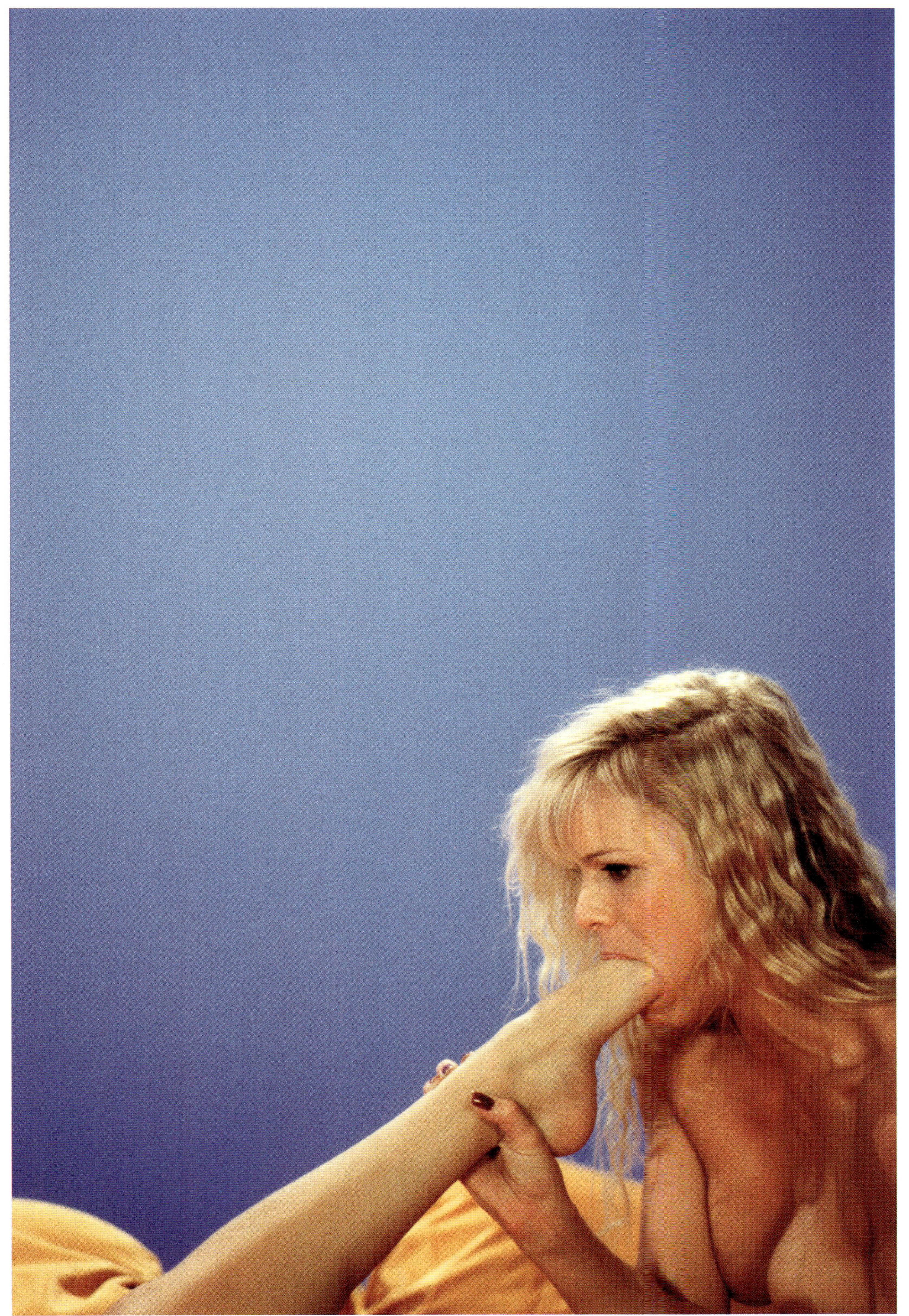

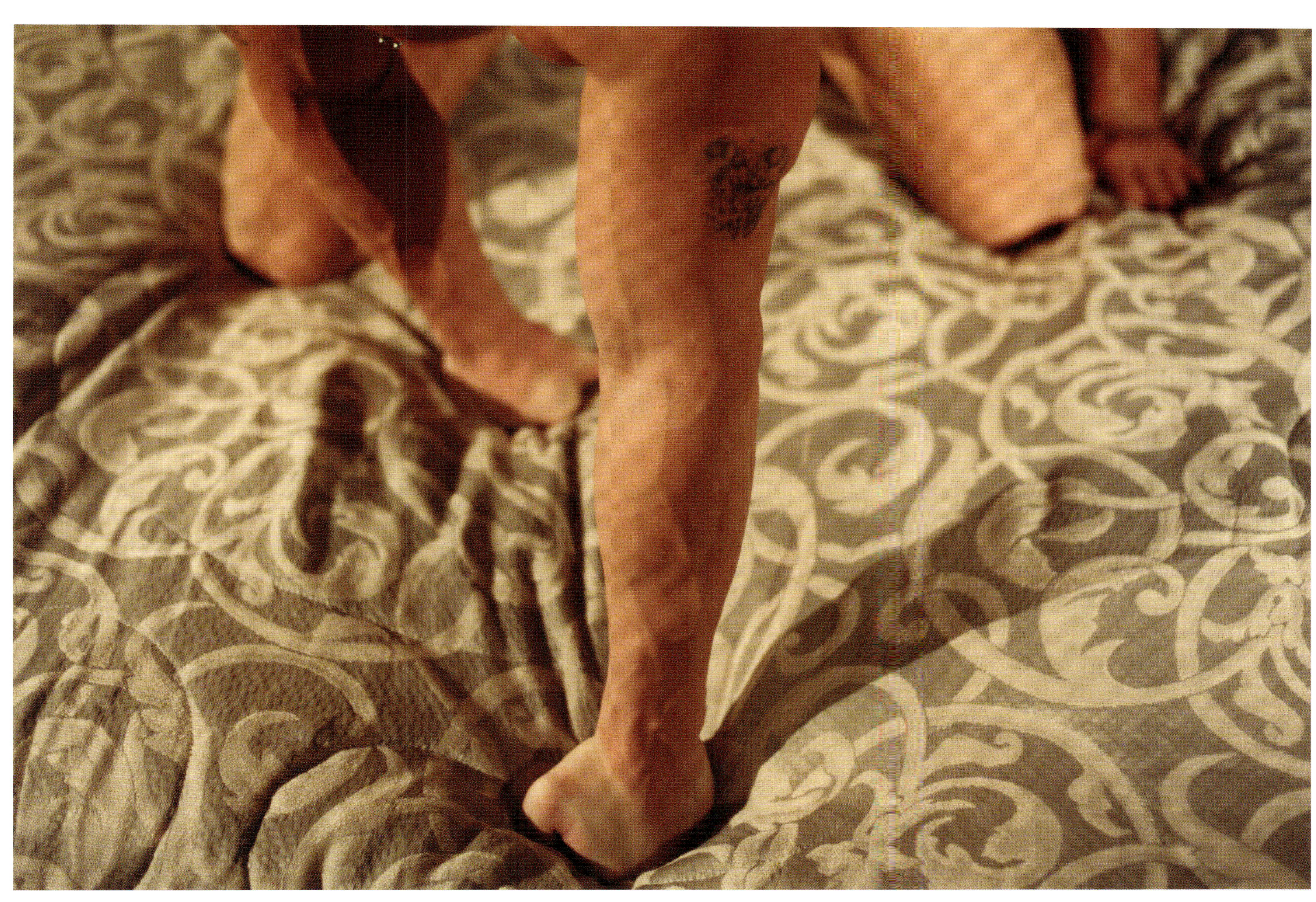

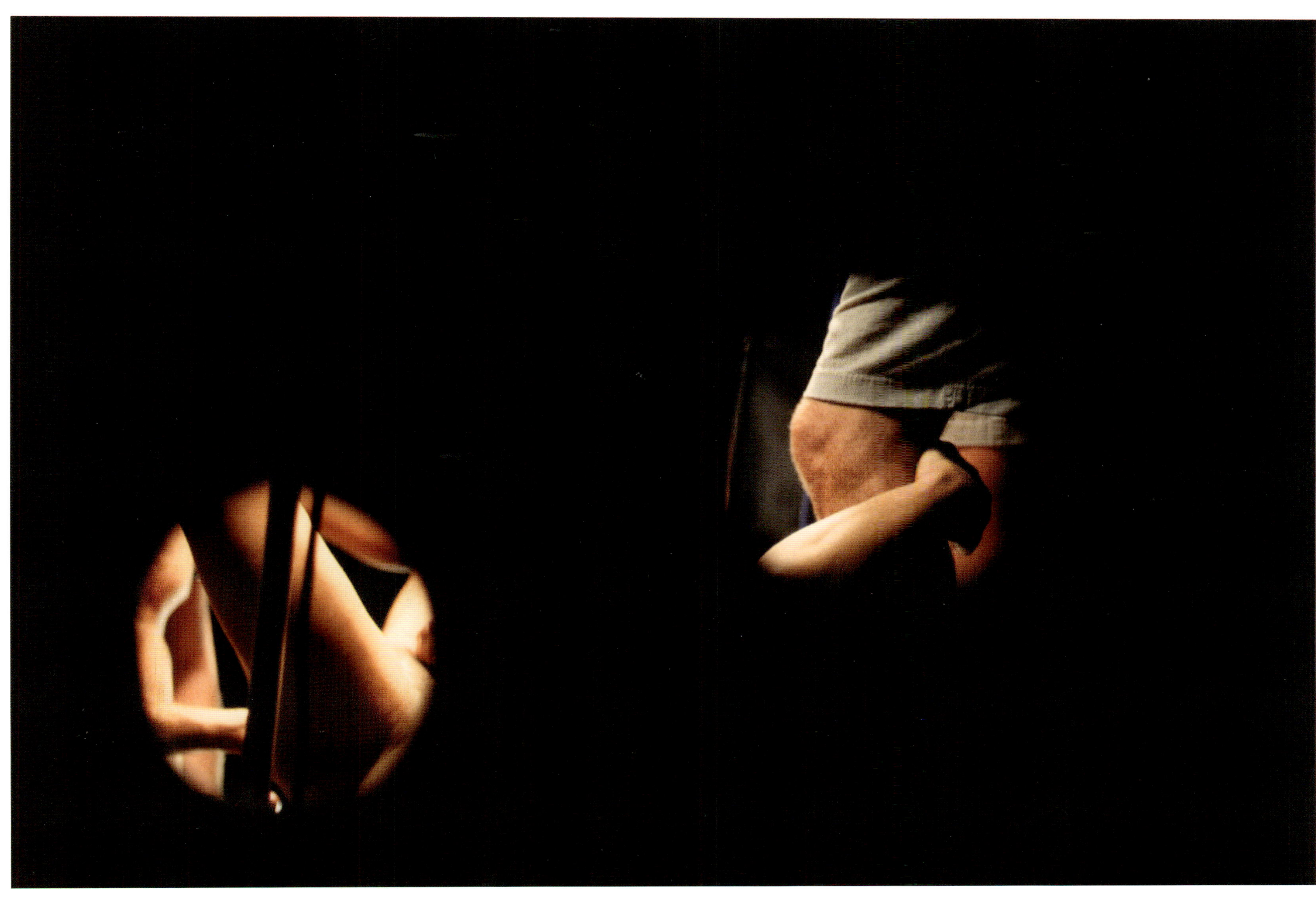

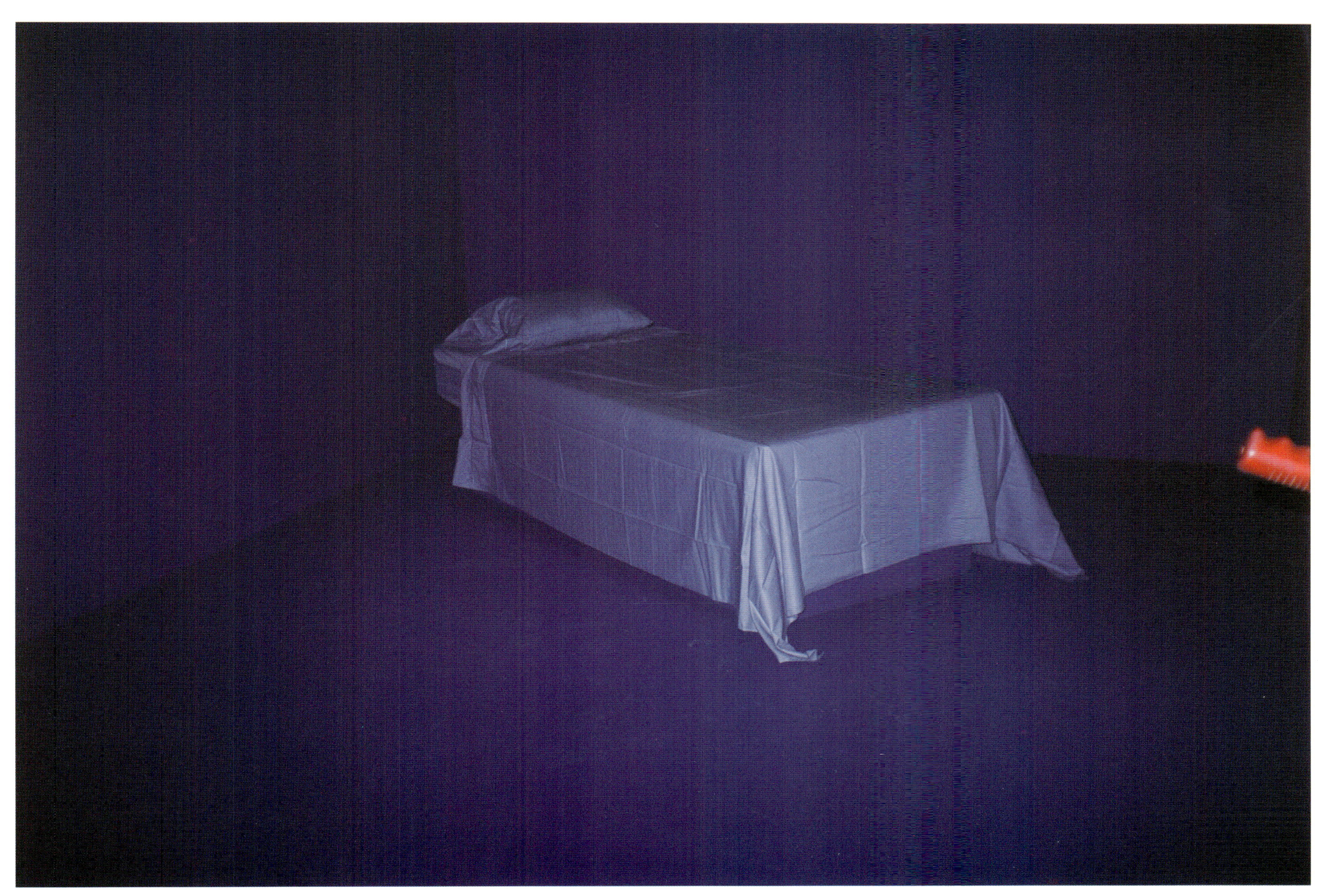

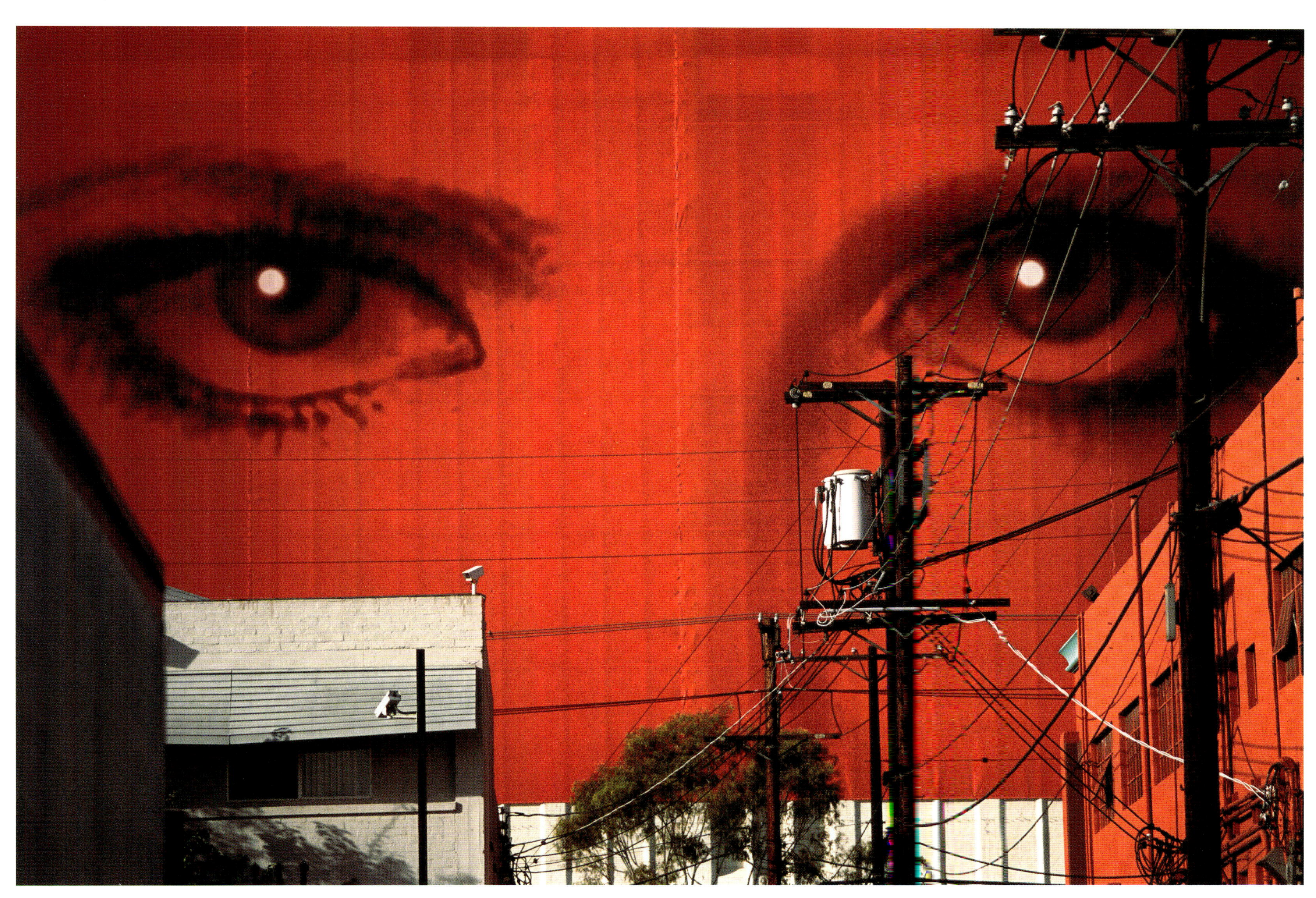

PORN MANIFESTO

I wanted to write a porn manifesto, but I'm not sure how.

That I'm more into porn than I'm into manifestoes might be the problem.

In porn, people use their own and others' bodies to try to prove their body's integrity, coherency — and fail.

JB pictures these tries.

People want to try to get to pleasure and stay there forever — and fail, want to know absolutely what they are, what a body is, or get rid of themselves forever in one volcanic self-shattering fuck — and fail.

JB takes pictures of these wants.

Like the porn stars they depict, his pictures work hard, which is also hard work but looks like "sex," i.e. pleasurable; easy; unthinking.

No one knows what a body is despite being in one, looking at its parts 24/7. Can't really see it all at once, your own or someone else's, which is part of the problem and causes the itch that needs to be scratched and the need to see pictures of the scratching. Sometimes this is embarrassing — nonknowledge of the body — and the reason some people find porn an embarrassment. At the video store renting the newest Caesar vid with some Bresson DVDs on top. At the newsstand yesterday with *Freshmen* and *Honcho* and a pack of cigarettes, I saw a guy buy *Wallpaper** so that he could tuck an issue of *Torso* inside of it. That porn is frequently associated with autoerotic rather than alloerotic pleasures intensifies embarrassment with condescension, pity. It is depressing that the regime of the couple has not been rethought, that relationality isn't more variegated.

It's hard to know exactly what a body is, what it's for, once you've watched a guy take most of an alert orange traffic cone inside him, fucking himself with its alertness until he shoots and moans with pleasure. It's hard to know what pleasure is when a traffic cone inside someone can be pleasurable, when watching a guy fit one inside him can be a turn-on.

Are you such a someone and/or are you the alert guy revealing usually private muscle control and erotic capacities?

It's hard to know what a body is because face fails to stay face; mouth and throat fail to be simply vocal; gag reflex fails to gag; arm fails to be arm; leg fails to remain leg; forearm and fist fail in their scale and their substantiality and are shown to be containable by rectum; inside fails to stay inside; outside fails to remain outside.

JB has taken photos in which it's hard to determine how many arms and legs a person has; how *horse-hung* doesn't quite describe a cock when its length is most of a chair's straight back. He takes pictures not so much to document sex acts as to observe the natural incomprehensibility of desire and intercourse too often occluded by the very terms used to describe it: *heterosexuality, homosexuality, fisting, doggy-style, horse-hung, etc.*

I've seen guys take inside them another guy's big arm almost up to the bicep and I don't know what that does to the concepts of inside and outside but it does something.

A performer—artist? sexualist?—buries his face deep into another performer's ass beneath the spray of a waterfall. The picture not only tests the meaning of *face* and *ass*, their metaphorical, alimentary connections, but also shows such an action, such attentive probing, one guy of another, to be as clarifying as water.

Face fails becomes seat; mouth fails becomes hole; gag reflex fails becomes pleasure filler. Body fails becomes "body."

Read this bodily failing as an allegory for art's relations with porn and vice versa. Can you any longer tell which is which, what is what? Do you care?

In his photos, JB tests art's gag reflex, makes art swallow, tracks these various body failures, develops them into something else. It's as if he figured out that art likes taking a traffic cone inside it and is able to show what that "looks like," what it feels like, while never simply depicting it. His carefully observed photos still porn action, attenuate its rush to turn-on, so that the strangeness of being turned on by not knowing what a body is can be looked at.

In porn, people also use their bodies to test any body's difference from or similarity to the objects and décor around it. Sometimes they swap positions with the inanimate. Sometimes the inanimate tops them. They find out what it's like to act like a commodity. Sometimes commodification tops them. Exchange value determines their ontology.

JB's earlier work drew attention to the inanimate's participation in erotic scenes—even the inanimate's creation of the erotic scene, the inanimate's dominance, its topping the human erotic. White sock and sneaker on the leg raised in the beige living room; "French" painting as witness to a fuck scene. The earlier work trafficked in observing how art and décor objects and guys fucking pushed each other in and out of focus. JB's most recent work clarifies such irreconcilability by bringing relations between bodies fucking and their decorative surroundings into sharp focus, thereby using both the soft-focus look of "gentlemen's" erotica and the high-gloss look of hardcore porn as his vernacular (but for different results).

Unlike most contemporary photography and video—art and commercial—porn is not a genre that dotes on technological special effects. While digital manipulation has become ubiquitous almost everywhere else (to the point of determining cinematic narrative), porn's economy and purpose (getting its viewers off) demand it remain at least partially, well, "documentary"—which is a loaded term but also a term with a big load porn is interested in releasing. JB has profited from working in the porn industry since 1989, toeing its seemingly paradoxical strict docu-aesthetic line: he never crops his photographs, nor are they ever manipulated; any staging is the result of the labor and art direction already available at the scene on the set. With his photos he puts up a mirror to the concepts of "staged" and "documentary"—reflecting both but not exactly either. He observes porn demanding documentary shoot its wad (glamour) and paying for it ("money shot").

Although Viagra and other pharmaceuticals have tampered with porn's documentary "purity"; although porn star bods are intensely groomed (shaved, tanned, waxed), pimply infelicities magically hidden with makeup, and physiques built with strict workout regimes (hyperbolized with steroids or not), most of the male porn stars don't partake of whatever would be the cosmetic implant equivalent usually de rigueur for the women in the industry. Biceps like rectal muscles can be trained, but cocks are the size they are. Some bodies are born for porn and become for a while porn somebodies.

Collisions of styles (faux Louis XVI, French Colonial, mid-century moderne, swank eclecticism); textures (real ferns battling it out with horticultural wallpaper and bamboo fabric); types of bodies (smooth twinks, roid monsters, fratboys, daddies, tuffs, buxom babes) deliriously juxtaposed in porn are usually, somehow, sadly, never seen to be its point. JB's photos allow to be considered what it would mean for collision to be porn's point.

I have a videotape of Bob Mizer at work during an early '80s AMG shoot. Over forty years in the biz of picturing men trying to achieve some fantasy or ideal of what men are to and for men, by that time, Mizer'd been anything but miserly, cataloguing countless beauties: marines on leave, drop-out jocks, bodybuilders, gas station attendants and drifters transformed into pharaohs and Greek gods, all demonstrating the inexhaustible erotic range of male flesh. The intensity to Bob Mizer's pursuit, his desire, can be seen in his look, his looking. His looking says something like:"They just keep coming. So many to take pictures of. Never enough time to take pictures of them, never enough film to take pictures of them, never enough light to match their light, which is why I sometimes go for gaudy carnival effects. They arrive for various reasons—from cachet to just cash. Some save it, others party and play and fade away. But before they fade who knows where I've taken their picture, written down their name."

Bob Mizer turned a truly amateur occupation into the prototype of an industry; JB returns the industry to the strangeness of guys embodying some transhistorical or ahistorical urge to see and be seen by one another.

Bob Mizer's Athletic Model Guild studios were the start of the yellow brick road of gay porn whose Oz is now everywhere.

JB's pictures are most "artistic" when they're most pornographic; most explicit or "pornographic" when they're most art. Art and porn sixty-nine for him so that he can document how the bodies of fantasy, which depend upon real bodies and their decorated surroundings, entice some to begin to consider what they are and how fantasy works.

It looks as unsafe as fantasy can be. Should be.

I could mention Atget and Brassai's prostitutes, Arbus's human extravagances, Karlheinz Weinberger's Teutonic gangs, Danny Lyons's bikers to give JB's project some kind of aesthetic pedigree, but I would hate to have to. Even though it might be helpful to say that, like Atget, he's labored with the community he commits to film, that his "Paris" is Hollywood and its shadow industry's locales, and that his pictures work like documents—between categories—I would hate to have to. I would like his photos to complicate the entire notion of aesthetic pedigree, properness, because too infrequently has art been demanded for its porn pedigree despite its centuries plumbing the sexual and erotic.

The first gay bar JB ever went to was called The Other Place; its acronym would be TOP. His photographs work in an other place, neither simply porn nor art but topping both.

Despite the ravishing gorgeousness—flawless skin, musculature, Technicolor hues—of the goings-on in JB's work, it would be a mistake to curb the erotic rush and illicit thrill and potential embarrassment of the pornographic barebacking his entire project, any prophylactic jettisoned in what he does to the aesthetic.

BRUCE HAINLEY, 2005

Acknowledgments: Amy Adler, Larry Barth, Chuck Billen, Victoria Brynner and Stardust Visions, Tony Duran, Chi Chi LaRue, Gary L'Heureux, Marcello Navarra, Rick Pirro, John Rutherford and COLT Studio Group, VCA, Corina Van De Vyvere

A Special Thanks to: Alex Vanagas for his enthusiasm and assistance in realizing this book, Bruce Hainley for his illuminations, John Weldon and Mike Keeler at Weldon Color Lab for their excellent work, Jack Woody and Axel Ziegler at Twin Palms Publishers for their commitment, perseverance, and attention to this project, and the performers for whom I have great admiration.

Jeff Burton

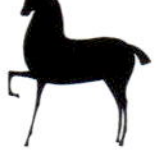

TWIN PALMS PUBLISHERS

Post Office 10229   Santa Fe, NM 87504   1.800.797.0680   www.twinpalms.com